TOXIC LEAK!

AN EVENT-BASED SCIENCE MODULE

TOXIC LEAK!

STUDENT EDITION

Russell G. Wright

D1518517

Dale Seymour Publications®

The developers of Event-Based Science have been encouraged and supported at every step in the creative process by the Superintendent and Board of Education of Montgomery County Public Schools, Rockville, Maryland (MCPS). The superintendent and board are committed to the systemic improvement of science instruction, grades preK–12. EBS is one of many projects undertaken to ensure the scientific literacy of *all* students.

The developers of *Toxic Leak!* pay special tribute to the editors, publisher, and reporters of the *Charlotte Observer*, the *Cecil Whig*, and *USA Today*. Without their cooperation and support the creation of this module would not have been possible.

Cover Photograph: © 1994 *Charlotte Observer*, Laura Mueller
Pages 2, 7, 9 *Charlotte Observer;* 11, 19 C. Doebler; 21 NASA; 26 and all "Student Voices" photographs Judy Kidd

Managing Editor: Cathy Anderson
Project Editor: Katarina Stenstedt
Production: Leanne Collins
Design Manager: Jeff Kelly
Text and Cover Design: Frank Loose Design, Portland, Oregon

This book is published by Dale Seymour Publications®, an imprint of Addison Wesley Longman, Inc.

This material is based upon work supported by the National Science Foundation under grant number MDR-9154094. Any opinions, findings, conclusions, or recommendations expressed in this publication are those of the Event-Based Science Project and do not necessarily reflect the views of the National Science Foundation.

Contents

Preface

The Event-Based Science Model

Toxic Leak! is a student booklet about ground-water that follows the Event-Based Science (EBS) Instructional Model. You will begin by watching "live" television news coverage and reading newspaper reports about leaking gasoline storage tanks that have contaminated wells in Paw Creek, North Carolina. Your discussions about the leaks and the well contamination will show you and your teacher that you already know a lot about the earth-science concepts in this event. Next, a real-world task puts you and your classmates in the roles of "homeowners" who must use scientific knowledge and processes to deal with a leak in your community. You will probably need more information before you start the task. If you do, *Toxic Leak!* provides hands-on activities and a variety of reading materials to give you some of the background you need. About half-way through the unit, you will be ready to begin the task. You will spend the rest of the time in this unit working on that task.

Scientific Literacy

Today, a literate citizen is expected to know more than how to read, write, and do simple arithmetic. Today, literacy includes knowing how to analyze problems, ask critical questions, and explain events. A literate citizen must also be able to apply scientific knowledge and processes in new situations. Event-Based Science allows you to practice these skills by placing the study of science in a meaningful context.

Knowledge cannot be transferred to your mind from the mind of your teacher, or from the pages of a textbook. Nor can knowledge occur in isolation from the other things you know about and have experienced in the real world. The Event-Based Science model is based on the idea that the

best way to know something is to be actively engaged in it.

Therefore, the Event-Based Science model simulates real-life events and experiences to make your learning more authentic and memorable. First, the event is brought to life through television news coverage. Viewing the news allows you to be there "as it happened," and that is as close as you can get to actually experiencing the event. Second, by simulating the kinds of teamwork and problem solving that occur every day in our work places and communities, you will experience the role that scientific knowledge and teamwork play in the lives of ordinary people. Thus *Toxic Leak!* is built around simulations of real-life events and experiences that affected people's lives and environments dramatically.

In an Event-Based Science classroom, you become the workers, your product is a solution to a real problem, and your teacher is your coach, guide, and advisor. You will be assessed on how you use scientific processes and concepts to solve problems and on the quality of your work.

One of the primary goals of the EBS Project is to place the learning of science in a real-world context and to make scientific learning fun. You should not allow yourself to become frustrated. If you cannot find a specific piece of information, it's okay to be creative.

Student Resources

Toxic Leak! is unlike a regular textbook. An Event-Based Science module tells a story about a real event; it has real newspaper articles about the event, and inserts that explain the scientific concepts involved in the event. It also contains science activities for you to conduct in your science class and activities that you may do in English, math, or social studies classes. In addition, an Event-Based Science module gives you and your classmates a real-world task to do. The task is always done by teams of students, with each team member performing a real-life role, while completing an important part of the task. The task cannot be completed without you and everyone else on your team doing their parts. The team approach allows you to share your knowledge and strengths. It also helps you learn to work with a team in a real-world situation. Today, most professionals work in teams.

Interviews with people who actually deal with problems like the one in your task are scattered throughout the Event-Based Science module. Middle school students who actually experienced the event tell their stories throughout the module too.

Since this module is unlike a regular textbook, you have much more flexibility in using it.

- You may read **The Story** for enjoyment or to find clues that will help you tackle your part of the task.

- You may read selections from the **Discovery File** when you need help understanding something in the story or when you need help with the task.

- You may read all the **On the Job** features because you are curious about what professionals do, or you may read only the interview with the professional who works in the role you've chosen because it may give you ideas that will help you complete the task.

- You may read the **In the News** features because they catch your eye, or as part of your search for information.

- You will probably read all the **Student Voices** features because they are interesting stories told by middle-school students like yourself.

This Event-Based Science module is also unlike regular textbooks because the collection of resources found in it is not meant to be complete. You must find additional information from other sources too. Textbooks, encyclopedias, maps, pamphlets, magazine and newspaper articles, videos, films, filmstrips, computer databases, and people in your community are all potential sources of useful information. It is vital to your preparation as a scientifically literate citizen of the twenty-first century that you get used to finding information on your own.

The shape of a new form of science education is beginning to emerge, and the Event-Based Science Project is leading the way. We hope you enjoy your experience with this module as much as we enjoyed developing it.

—Russell G. Wright, Ed.D.
Project Director and Principal Author

Problems with Groundwater

Water is the basis of our lives. Our very existence on planet Earth depends on this most precious and limited resource. Here are a few basic, important facts to soak up.

Nearly seventy-five percent (75%) of the earth is covered by water, found mostly in the oceans. But did you know that just three percent (3%) of Earth's total water is *fresh water* (water that contains very little salt)? Of that three percent, most is locked in the north and south polar caps in the form of ice. The remaining fresh water is underground.

You would think that on a planet as large as Earth, with seventy-five percent of its surface covered with water, we would have plenty to drink. But we don't. In what could be called the "trickle down" principle of *hydrologic* (water) science, less than one percent of available water is suitable for drinking. Indeed, water is a priceless natural resource.

As the twenty-first century draws closer, we have begun to reflect on the many ways we use water. We use it to produce electric power; we use it in agriculture; we use it for industrial purposes; and we use it for our personal needs. To understand just one of the many reasons people are concerned about the future of our water supply, you must look underground.

Groundwater, the water stored beneath the earth's surface, is the source of over half of the fresh water available for drinking in the United States. About ninety-six percent (96%) of rural areas—the small towns distant from major cities—depend on groundwater as their main source of fresh water.

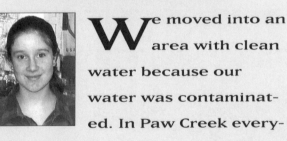

STUDENT VOICES

We moved into an area with clean water because our water was contaminated. In Paw Creek everyone had his or her well checked, and now is using bottled water until city water is put in.

JENNY SMITH
PAW CREEK, NC

With America's growing population, expanding cities, and flourishing industrial areas, it is clear that our cherished freshwater supply is under great stress. One of the polluting sources may be as close as the gasoline storage tanks under your neighborhood gas station. Consider them underground time bombs.

About 1.6 million underground petroleum storage tanks dot the nation from coast to coast. Many of these tanks were placed in the ground as far back as the 1950s, some even earlier.

Large petroleum tank farms or simple "mom-and-pop" gasoline stations—both sites have the potential of a gasoline leak that could contaminate surface water and groundwater or cause fires and explosions. Gasoline seepage can put people in contact with substances able to cause serious health problems. If gasoline is consumed by even a healthy person, the result can be anemia, brain damage, other nervous system disorders, or kidney failure. Experiments with laboratory animals have shown that benzene, one of the 400 compounds found in gasoline, causes cancer. Gasoline is the most toxic substance that ordinary people encounter day after day.

Take note. *An estimated 100,000 fuel tanks in the United States alone already leak!* Tens of millions of gallons of gasoline are released each year. And it only takes one gallon of gasoline a day entering groundwater to contaminate the drinking water supply for 50,000 people.

➤ continued on page 2

➤ continued from page 1

But these are statistics; reality can be as close as the headline in a newspaper. ■

Discussion Questions

1. What is groundwater?

2. What are some of the ways that water can move through the ground?

3. Where does your drinking water come from?

4. How do you know your drinking water is safe to drink?

5. Could your water be contaminated by gasoline leaking from a storage tank or by any other source of contamination?

6. What other things might contaminate water?

IN THE NEWS

Leaked gasoline shadows neighbors' lives

■ Fuel never cleaned up, and cancer cases among residents worry this Charlotte neighborhood.

By JOHN HECHINGER and MARY ELIZABETH DeANGELIS
Staff Writers

Twelve years ago, more than 100,000 gallons of gasoline leaked from an Amoco storage tank towering over Charlotte's Paw Creek community.

No one knows exactly how much.

No one knows exactly how far the gas has spread since then.

But one thing the company and the government do know: To this day, no one has cleaned up the leak.

It's a dangerous pattern.

Since the 1960s, oil companies at Paw Creek spilled at least 600,000 gallons of gasoline and other fuels, state records show. That's enough to fill the gas tanks of 50,000 Ford Escorts.

Until the late 1980s, the state did little to make oil firms clean up those spills, which still taint water deep below ground. In only three cases did state regulators issue fines.

Gasoline City: Residents, who once accepted their industrial neighbors, worry the tanks have hurt their health. Gas companies say there's no evidence residents have been harmed.

Paw Creek leaks

Documented fuel leaks at Paw Creek community since 1960. In gallons, minimum estimate.

Company	Estimated gallons
Colonial Pipeline	242,000
Exxon	120,000
Amoco	100,000
Citgo	75,000
Others	63,000
TOTAL	**600,000**

SOURCE: N.C. Division of Environmental Management

GEORGE BREISACHER/Staff

Last month, N.C. cancer experts released a report that shocked Paw Creek: In the northwest Charlotte community, they found double the normal level of leukemia, the deadly bone-marrow cancer.

From 1987 to 1990, scientists studied the northwest Mecklenburg region including Paw Creek. Out of about 25,000 people, they found 10 cases of leukemia; investigators expected five, based on the county average.

Chemicals in gasoline are known to cause cancer. Now, the state plans to study Paw Creek further to try to determine whether there's a link between the cancer and the gasoline.

The high leukemia count could be a fluke, a statistical blip. Oil companies and government officials say there's no evidence that tank farms caused the community's cancer.

Please see Gasoline/page 3A

THE CHARLOTTE OBSERVER, JUNE 20, 1993

Gasoline

Continued from page 2A

Meanwhile, the people of Paw Creek are scared and angry.

Sam Killman Jr., 75, lives in a red brick house across from Amoco's gleaming white oil tanks. In 1987, his doctor told him he had leukemia.

"If I spilled oil and didn't clean it up, they'd put me in jail," said Killman. "The companies always talk about needing more time — well, how much more time are they going to get?"

Some oil companies admit they've had environmental problems at Paw Creek.

For example, Amoco waited at least a year before reporting its 1981 spill to the state. Then, after removing some of the gasoline, the company stopped most of its cleanup efforts in the late 1980s.

"It was a major mistake," Amoco spokesman Jim Spangler said of the 1981 spill and cleanup delay. "It is something we're not proud of. It is certainly not the way we operate today."

Pipeline fuels tank farms

For decades, people at Paw Creek accepted their industrial neighbors. Every day, they drove by four-story oil tanks emblazoned with familiar names: Amoco, BP, Citgo, Exxon, Shell.

About 3,600 people live within a mile of the tank farms, or fuel-storage terminals. Near the intersection of Freedom Drive and Old Mount Holly Road, it's a city of gasoline.

At Paw Creek, 13 oil companies operate terminals that can store 128 million gallons of fuel.

The terminals draw gas from pipelines that snake underground from the Gulf of Mexico to the Northeast. Tanker trucks pull into the terminals to pick up fuel for gas stations.

Neighbors at Paw Creek now know that deadly chemicals lurk in gasoline. Even small quantities can cause cancer if a person is exposed over years. Exposure can come from drinking tainted water or breathing contaminated air.

One of those chemicals, called benzene, is a major part of gasoline and an especially potent cancer-causing agent, government scientists say.

But it's tough to prove a link between an environmental hazard and a particular community's cancer rate. Research requires years of careful detective work and may never be conclusive.

Experts caution that cancer is common, usually related to smoking, diet and family health history. And the people of Paw Creek may have been exposed to cancer-causing chemicals elsewhere.

"We've made conclusions to continue to watch," said Tim Aldrich, director of the N.C. cancer surveillance unit and author of the Paw Creek cancer study. "We haven't ruled anything out, but we haven't ruled anything in."

Paw Creek oil companies downplay the problem. They say workers at refineries and terminals across the country — those at greatest risk — haven't shown higher rates of illness.

"I think it's probably the fear of the unknown," said Jay Scrivner, an Amoco environmental engineer. "Boy, you mention cancer these days — it's become a very scary subject. But I think it's speculative. We need to know more facts."

No danger seen in fumes

Two government agencies oversee the protection of Mecklenburg's environment.

In general, the N.C. Division of Environmental Management's office in Mooresville is responsible for protecting Mecklenburg County's water. In some cases, the county has a role.

Mecklenburg's Department of Environmental Protection is supposed to keep an eye on the air, making inspections and responding to complaints.

This summer, the county plans to mount an intensive study, taking air samples near the terminals.

Top county environmental officials say people in Paw Creek don't need to worry about tainted water or polluted air.

"It's more of a nuisance than anything else," said John Barry, director of the county's Department of Environmental Protection. "If you live near a gasoline terminal, you will expect to have some gasoline odors, just like if you live near a fertilizer plant, you'll have fertilizer odors — it's just one of those things."

"I don't see any danger in it," he added. "I see probably no more danger in that than in putting gas in your car."

The county says companies generally follow air-quality laws. But water is a different story. State and county records show a long history of oil-company violations.

The Observer reviewed hundreds of pages of environmental documents. They show that:

■ In 18 leaks, Paw Creek oil companies spilled 600,000 gallons of gasoline and other fuels. by conservative estimates. In nine others, no one knows how much fuel spilled into the ground.

■ Since 1987, environmental officials sampled about 80 drinking wells in the Paw Creek area and found 17 with contamination.

Investigators found two tainted with gasoline or gasoline byproducts. The others contained solvents, often used to clean trucks or in the dry-cleaning industry. Regulators still don't know the source of the contamination.

Mecklenburg officials don't know how many people in Paw Creek still use wells. They say they're confident that no one is drinking contaminated water. They've connected the 17 homes with tainted wells to city water supplies.

Still, residents fear they may have been drinking from polluted wells years ago.

■ In 170 cases since 1991, oil companies violated their permits for discharging wastewater into streams.

In 38 instances, companies released water with contamination above state limits. In 132 other cases, firms didn't properly document their discharges, as they are required to do by law.

In 27 known leaks, few fines

The state has rarely punished the Paw Creek oil companies.

For the 27 known fuel leaks, the state fined only three companies: Amoco, Citgo and Exxon. The first fine came in 1991. Combined, their penalties totaled less than $45,000. The maximum fine is $10,000 a day; in some cases, the state could have fined more than $1 million.

Last December, Amoco paid its first fine for the 1981 spill: $27,700 for missing a cleanup deadline. The state had recommended $44,200. But the N.C. Division of Environmental Management agreed to cut that amount after Amoco protested.

Brenda Smith, supervisor of the state's Mooresville environmental office since 1989, is responsible for monitoring and enforcing laws about groundwater pollution.

"Looking at it, knowing what we could have fined them, and how much money the companies have, the fines may seem minuscule," Smith said. "But they're in line with fines the state has given to companies in comparable situations."

Smith also conceded that the state didn't always push hard enough for oil companies to clean up their spills.

In the early 1980s, she said, few people or companies had today's awareness of environmental hazards. Smith said the office was understaffed. Five years ago, the state had only three staffers keeping track of 71 known cases of groundwater contamination in 12 N.C counties.

Now, the number of groundwater regulators has quadrupled, and Smith said the state is pushing hard to make sure Paw Creek gets cleaned up.

"We're better staffed," Smith said. "If you had the same spills you had 10 years ago today, you'd have a very different response from everyone involved. I feel very certain of that."

The people of Paw Creek hope so.

Kathy Cloninger, 52, a retired postal clerk and mother of three, lives less than half a mile from the tanks. Her hair thin from chemotherapy, she suffers from uterine, lung and lymph node cancer.

"The main thing we need to do is get the oil companies to do something," Cloninger said. "It's too late for me, but let's hope we can get something done for future generations."

Cleanup is expensive, slow

Oil companies say they're spending millions to clean up environmental damage and install the most up-to-date pollution control equipment.

"It's our job as good, responsible corporate citizens to get in there and clean up the past problems we may have had," said John DuPre, who oversees Exxon's Paw Creek terminal and others across the southeast and west.

Terminal managers say cleanup often drags on because identifying and removing contamination requires extensive study.

The firms say required state regulatory approval slows down the process. Amoco, for example, hopes to finish cleanup of the 1981 spill in five or six years.

"Unfortunately, it seems to take forever," said James Utke, Citgo's Charlotte terminal manager. "I feel the same way. We would like nothing more than to find a spill, know what it is and take it out of the ground."

The Toxic War in Paw Creek

The residents of Paw Creek, a community in the northwest section of Charlotte, North Carolina, have accepted being called "a gasoline city."

Nearly 3,600 residents of Paw Creek live within a mile of fuel storage terminals owned and operated by 13 different oil companies. The tanks have been part of the community's landscape, a familiar sight mixed in with the churches, banks, and stores. The four-story tall tanks proudly display such familiar names as Shell, Exxon, Colonial Pipeline, Amoco, and Citgo. All together, the tanks can hold nearly 130 million gallons of gasoline and other fuels.

In 1981, as it was later learned, Amoco experienced a leak from the bottom of a 40-year-old storage tank at the Paw Creek terminal. An estimated 100,000 gallons of gasoline leaked from the ruptured fuel storage tank into the ground.

That wasn't the only spill either. Several other companies had experienced similar problems at the Paw Creek terminal. It was eventually determined that since the 1960s, at least 600,000 gallons of gasoline and other fuels had seeped below ground from 18 separate leaks. That's enough to fill 60 gasoline-tank trucks. Some of the leaked

STUDENT VOICES

My friends were sick. Some of them developed blisters. Now we are on city water, and we use a water filter, too. I think people should be more careful with our natural resources.

KELLY HAYES
CHARLOTTE, NC

We smelled gasoline in the air, and our water contained gasoline. We decided to move away from Paw Creek. A lot of people want to move, but can't sell their homes.

DESMOND J. STOWE
PAW CREEK, NC

fuels had been recovered, but much of it could not be reclaimed.

Starting in the mid-1980s, townspeople noticed odd odors in the air on hot, summer days. Others detected curious smells coming from tap water drawn from faucets connected to their underground wells. The water had a strange taste, too. Despite these signs, most people in the community believed their observations deserved no special attention. They thought that if something were wrong, they would have been told of the problem.

Finally, the invisible war taking place in this small community produced its first casualties. Unexplained illnesses began to be reported. Blisters in the mouth and on the tongue, lips, and throat were common. One doctor told a patient suffering with blisters that he had never seen anything like it before. Seemingly healthy individuals began to be stricken by cancer of the hips, back, and lungs, along with other illnesses. Deaths in Paw Creek from leukemia and various cancers appeared to be on the increase.

In 1992 a report explained that North Carolina state health officials had found twice the normal level of leukemia in the area. A survey of Paw Creek residents also found a high number of other cancers. County health officials sampled some 80 wells, finding 17 of them contaminated, and 2 of them fouled by gasoline or gasoline by-products.

While the danger signs seemed obvious, state and county environmental officials moved slowly. To the residents of Paw Creek, the time-consuming battle over data and statistics seemed irrelevant. For instance, disagreements centered over "environment-related" versus "lifestyle-related" cancers. Scientists, environmentalists, and oil company officials debated whether there was a link between tank spills and the known health problems. Each side brought to the debate information to support its own beliefs and viewpoints. Paw Creek residents accused health officials of keeping them in the dark about the tainted wells and potential health hazards. Officials from the oil companies and the government claimed that no evidence supported a cause and effect relationship between the leaking tank farm and the community's heightened medical problems.

People living near the leaking tanks had their quiet neighborhoods turned into blocks of fear. Arguments among government and oil company officials seemed like foot dragging to residents whose loved ones and neighbors were stricken with cancer. As Paw Creek continues to deal with its environmental plight, it is but one example of what many people fear may become an epidemic of groundwater pollution incidents throughout the country. ∎

Paw Creek water options debated

■ Council member says Charlotte should extend service because of dangers from leaks, and worry about costs later.

By BRUCE HENDERSON
Staff Writer

The city should immediately extend water to Paw Creek residents worried over the safety of their well water and decide who's going to pay for it later, a Charlotte City Council member said Monday.

"Which is more important: to let people suffer for two more years, or go ahead and do something about it?" said at-large council member Don Reid.

Since the 1960s, oil storage tanks in the northwest Charlotte neighborhood have leaked into the ground at least 600,000 gallons of gasoline and other fuel. A 1992 state study found twice the normal level of leukemia in the area, and residents say their community suffers a disproportionate number of other cancers.

Until this month, many residents say local and state officials never told them about the extent of the contamination.

A leader of a Paw Creek citizens' group applauded Reid's proposal, on which discussion was postponed until the council's next meeting. But he said the oil companies should pay for bringing clean water to his neighborhood.

"I want them all to jump in and do what's right," said David Scott, vice president of the Paw Creek Health and Safety Association. "I don't think the city taxpayers should carry this burden. They're not the ones who did this, really. The oil companies should be responsible."

Residents last Friday met directly with representatives of five oil companies that have storage facilities in Paw Creek.

Some of the company representatives were "hearing from the community for the first time what their concerns were," said council member Hoyle Martin, whose district includes Paw Creek.

Last Thursday and Friday, Charlotte-Mecklenburg Utilities Department workers blanketed the contaminated area with fliers describing how residents can connect to city water lines.

CMUD Director Joe Stowe said nearly 1,000 fliers were distributed door to door and in churches within an area about 2 miles in diameter. By Monday afternoon, about 25 people had called the department for more information, Stowe said. Four applied for water connections and one for an extension of a water main.

If homeowners have to pay for the hookups, the cost would be substantial — $808 to connect to an existing water main, or $738 to extend a main along a street. The $738 fee applies to customers whose wells are contaminated.

Low-interest bank loans and a no-interest loan fund, based on need, are available to help pay for the work.

That's not good enough during a "real emergency," said council member Reid. Reid, seconded by Martin, moved that the city install lines now to Paw Creek residents who want city water.

"I don't know what the problem is, but you don't have to be a geologist to know something's wrong," Reid said. "Why don't we do what's right and figure out a way to pay for it later?"

THE CHARLOTTE OBSERVER, JUNE 29, 1993

A SPECIAL REPORT: PAW CREEK'S CANCER SCARE

People fear cancers are linked to gas leaks

■ Neighborhood pride now mixes uneasily with health concerns as families share stories about disease.

By MARY ELIZABETH DeANGELIS And JOHN HECHINGER
Staff Writers

Pam Scott grew up climbing trees, splashing in streams and drinking the water in her Paw Creek neighborhood.

Her family lived in a green frame house on Tom Sadler Road, and later she and her husband moved into a yellow one right behind it.

She used to love living in the northwest Charlotte community, with its old shade trees, flowered bushes and well-kept homes.

Now she's afraid it's killing her. She has cancer.

In Paw Creek, many share Scott's fear.

They know what the experts have told them: There's no proof that nearby oil companies caused their cancer. Cancer is common. It might be in their family's history. It could come from smoking, their jobs, their diet.

Then, they take another look at the huge fuel tanks, as familiar in Paw Creek as its churches and community stores.

They remember the gasoline that leaked into the ground while many were still drinking from wells.

They remember a sickly-sweet odor on a warm summer's day.

They remember their neighbors who got sick, and the names add up in their heads.

A reporter spoke with 27 families who live on Scott's street. Over the past decade, 12 homes had someone with cancer.

Many don't seem much of a mystery: a longtime smoker who died of lung cancer, an elderly man with prostate cancer, a middle-aged woman with breast cancer.

Recalling a funny smell

But what about Pam Scott?

She's 35 and the mother of a 3-year-old. Cancer has invaded her lung and hip.

She lives about a third of a mile from the terminals.

"I used to feel safe out here," she said. "Now I feel like it's dangerous to anybody who's lived out here for any period of time."

Scott worked in a real estate office and seemed healthy. Then, in March, a throbbing pain in her shoulder forced her to the doctor.

Cancer was spreading through her body. Since then, she's lost 61 pounds. Chemotherapy has taken most of her brown hair. She can't

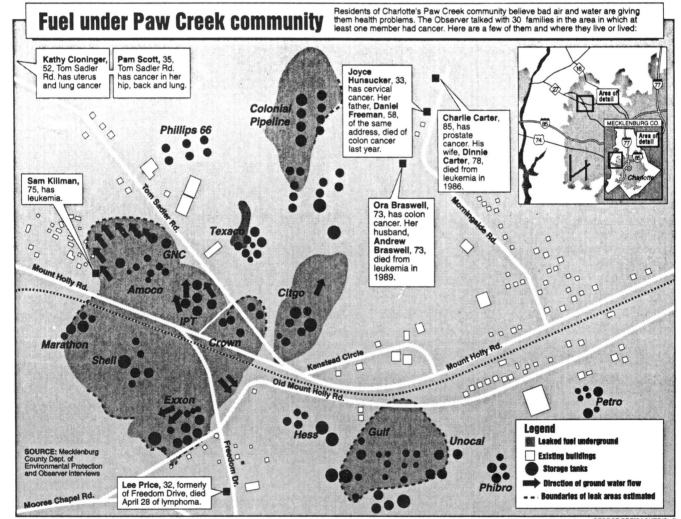

Fuel under Paw Creek community

Residents of Charlotte's Paw Creek community believe bad air and water are giving them health problems. The Observer talked with 30 families in the area in which at least one member had cancer. Here are a few of them and where they live or lived:

Kathy Cloninger, 52, Tom Sadler Rd. has uterus and lung cancer

Pam Scott, 35, Tom Sadler Rd. has cancer in her hip, back and lung.

Joyce Hunsucker, 33, has cervical cancer. Her father, **Daniel Freeman,** 58, of the same address, died of colon cancer last year.

Charlie Carter, 85, has prostate cancer. His wife, **Dinnie Carter,** 78, died from leukemia in 1986.

Sam Killman, 75, has leukemia.

Ora Braswell, 73, has colon cancer. Her husband, **Andrew Braswell,** 73, died from leukemia in 1989.

Colonial Pipeline

Phillips 66

Tom Sadler Rd.

Texaco

GNC

Mount Holly Rd.

Amoco

IPT

Citgo

Morningside Rd.

Marathon

Shell

Crown

Kenstead Circle

Mount Holly Rd.

Old Mount Holly Rd.

Exxon

Freedom Dr.

Hess

Gulf

Unocal

Petro

Phibro

SOURCE: Mecklenburg County Dept. of Environmental Protection and Observer interviews

Lee Price, 32, formerly of Freedom Drive, died April 28 of lymphoma.

Moores Chapel Rd.

16
27
77
Area of detail
I-85
MECKLENBURG CO.
74
77
Area of detail
85
Charlotte

Legend
■ Leaked fuel underground
□ Existing buildings
● Storage tanks
➡ Direction of ground water flow
--- Boundaries of leak areas estimated

GEORGE BREISACHER/Staff

THE CHARLOTTE OBSERVER, JUNE 20, 1993

give her son D.J. a bath because she's too weak to lift him into the tub.

"I get scared when I think about what's going to happen to me," she said as she sat in a chair in her bedroom and watched D.J. play. "I just don't feel like I'll get to see my son grow up. . . . "

Kathy Cloninger, 52, lives three houses away. It's about a half mile from the dozens of tanks that sit along the southeast end of Tom Sadler Road.

She's had two operations and chemotherapy for the cancer in her right lung and uterus. She doesn't smoke. On Thursday, she learned the cancer had spread again, this time to her lymph nodes.

"I remember in 1985 the water smelled and tasted funny," she said. "I thought, 'Surely if something was wrong, they'd tell us.' It's scary to think something you can't see is killing you."

Resident saw tanks built

At first, the shiny steel tanks intrigued Kathy Cloninger's husband, Bob. He was 5 when the men from Texas set up camp across the street from his house and started building what's now the Exxon terminal.

He'd sit on his front porch and watch them for hours.

"I was amazed by it, bringing in all that steel and laying it down," said Bob Cloninger, now 55. "And I remember smelling the fumes — it never bothered me."

It was the early 1940s, and the oil companies began using Paw Creek as the point where tanker trucks could fill up, then distribute their gasoline to service stations across the Carolinas.

"Most of the people that worked for the oil companies were good friends. A lot of the truck drivers went to our church," he said.

He joined the Navy and was stationed in Hawaii, where he met his wife. He brought her home in 1962 to Paw Creek, where the couple raised three children.

The two lived across the street from Exxon until 1969, when they moved to a larger, brick house.

He worked for the railroad. She was a postal clerk, until the cancer that started four years ago forced her to quit. He retired to take care of her.

"If only we knew then what we know now, we would have never left Hawaii," Bob Cloninger said.

Joyce Hunsucker, 33, wonders, too.

Her family has lived for 28 years on Morningside Road, lined with small houses and scattered mobile homes. Trees block the view of the nearby tanks.

Hunsucker has been treated for cervical cancer. Her father Daniel Freeman, 58, died last year of colon cancer.

"It seems like a lot of our old neighbors have died from cancer — and not all of them were old," Hunsucker said. "Like my dad, he had never been sick, he was so healthy, he never even got a cold."

"We have a creek in back and you could smell the gas. It smelled like rotten eggs. And the water looked like a rainbow; it had lots of different colors in it."

A block away, Ora Braswell, 73, has colon cancer. She's lived in her home for more than 20 years. In 1989, her husband, Andrew, a retired supervisor with the Air National Guard, died from leukemia.

Dinnie Carter, 78, a 40-year Morningside Road resident, died from leukemia in 1986. Her husband, Charlie, has prostate cancer.

"The tanks are right in back of me, we could smell them," Braswell said. "I think when people built them, they didn't know they were bad for the environment. It's just like smoking. Nobody told us it was dangerous to smoke back then."

Well water tainted

Sam Killman Jr. is surrounded.

A chain-link fence separates his backyard from Amoco's tanks. The front porch of his immaculate brick house overlooks Marathon Oil tanks.

When Killman and his wife, Elnora, moved to the house on Mount Holly Road in 1976, he didn't mind the view. He hauled gasoline for more than 30 years. It helped raise the couple's nine children, including Sam Killman III, the former Charlotte police chief.

But gasoline tainted Sam Killman Jr.'s drinking water. In 1987, he was diagnosed with leukemia.

Nobody knows when the chemicals leaked into his well. County testers found the contamination in late 1988.

Amoco, his next-door neighbor, paid Killman's $847 bill to hook up to city water.

"It's taken all my energy," said Killman, 75. "I love this house and I don't want to move."

Vernette Price, who lives on Rhyne Road, can't wait to get her 2-year-old son A.J. out of Paw Creek. Her husband Lee grew up about a quarter-mile from fuel terminals.

He died April 28 from lymphoma, a cancer of the lymphoid tissue. He was 32.

"My husband was never, ever sick," she said. "The only time he had ever been to a doctor was about a year and a half ago, when he was diagnosed with cancer."

The couple had lived about eight years in their large, neatly decorated mobile home when A.J. was born in 1991. They were saving for a house.

Then Lee Price, a telephone installer, started losing his energy.

"We were new parents and not getting a lot of sleep, so we thought it was natural," Vernette Price said. "He thought he might have pulled a muscle and when he didn't get better, they did a test, and found the tumor."

The next year, he lost his hair and appetite to chemotherapy treatments. Relatives took turns caring for A.J. while Vernette Price stayed with her husband in the hospital.

"It's just not normal for someone that healthy to get that sick," she said. "Something's not right."

"I get scared when I think about what's going to happen to me. I just don't feel like I'll get to see my son grow up."

— Pam Scott, pictured above with her husband, Fred, who is holding their 3-year-old son, D.J. Cancer has invaded her lung and hip. She is 35.

"I remember in 1985 the water smelled and tasted funny. I thought, 'Surely if something was wrong, they'd tell us.' It's scary to think something you can't see is killing you."

— Kathy Cloninger, at left with her husband, Bob. She's had two operations and chemotherapy for the cancer in her right lung and uterus. She doesn't smoke. Just Thursday, she learned the cancer has spread to her lymph nodes.

N.C. to probe handling of Paw Creek fuel leaks

By JOHN HECHINGER
And MARY ELIZABETH DeANGELIS
Staff Writers

North Carolina's top environmental official on Monday said he will investigate the state's handling of fuel leaks that contaminate Charlotte's Paw Creek community.

And some city and Mecklenburg County officials called for stepped-up efforts to clean up the neighborhood's environmental hazards.

Their comments came after The Observer reported Sunday that oil firms had leaked at least 600,000 gallons of gasoline and other fuels in Paw Creek since the 1960s.

Until the late 1980s, the state had done little to require cleanup of the spills, which still taint water deep underground.

A state study found a high number of leukemia cases in the area, and scientists are trying to find out whether there's a link to the pollution.

"We're taking this matter seriously," said Jonathan Howes, director of the N.C. Department of Environmental, Health and Natural Resources. "This is not a matter I want to toss off as though there's nothing there."

Howes said the state would consider buying people's contaminated property in the northwest Charlotte region if he determines that residents face serious health risks.

But Howes cautioned that such a move would be a last resort. For now, Howes said his Raleigh staff — perhaps with help from an independent consulting firm — would investigate the problem.

"Nothing about this had been brought to my attention," said Howes, an appointee of Gov. Jim

Paw Creek community

MECKLENBURG CO.

Area of detail

Charlotte

N

0   3
Miles

GEORGE BREISACHER/Staff

THE CHARLOTTE OBSERVER, JUNE 22, 1993

Officials call for stepped-up cleanup efforts

Hunt, who took office in January. "All of this is new to me and basically to all policy-level leadership in the department."

A spokeswoman for Hunt said the state "has a moral obligation to do all it can to protect Paw Creek families and to act as an environmental watchdog."

Thirteen oil companies operate tank farms, or fuel-storage terminals, at Paw Creek. Last month, a state cancer study of the area found twice the expected level of leukemia, the deadly bone-marrow cancer.

Chemicals in gasoline are known to cause cancer. The chemicals, including benzene, could have contaminated groundwater that supplies residents' wells. Fumes could be another route for exposure.

The high leukemia count could be a statistical fluke.

Oil companies and local government regulators say there's no evidence that tank farms caused the cancers of community residents. They say residents face no danger. Oil companies say they're doing everything they can to fix environmental problems.

On Monday, Parks Helms, Mecklenburg County commissioners chairman, called for better county staffing and funding of environmental protection.

"It is a disturbing revelation," Helms of Paw Creek's problems. "I think the whole community ought to be upset about it. I think we ought to proceed with dispatch to deal with it."

Joye   Martin

N.C. Rep. Billy Joye of Belmont, whose district includes Paw Creek, said: "I have to put myself in these people's shoes. If I lived there I wouldn't for sure feel that enough is being done."

City council member Hoyle Martin, who also represents Paw Creek, criticized John Barry, director of Mecklenburg County's Department of Environmental Protection.

"I'm a little concerned that Dr. Barry seems to belittle the residents' concerns," Martin said. "A man in his position should be more sensitive about what's happening in the community."

Barry defended his judgment: "I don't like to carry out enforcement actions through the news media," he said. "It's unfortunate that we can't do things as fast, and as neatly as the residents want us to. You cannot just snap your fingers and have the problems go away."

The people of Paw Creek weren't satisfied. "I feel angry with the state and the county and whoever else was responsible," said Kitty Brunk, 57, who grew up near the terminals and now owns two houses in the area. "They let it (gasoline) seep into the ground without making anyone clean it up."

❝ This is not a matter I want to toss off as though there's nothing here. ❞

— Jonathan Howes, director of the N.C. Department of Environment, Health and Natural Resources

Finding a Safe Water Supply

City Profile

Population: 729
Elevation: Sea level
Location: At the head of Chesapeake Bay

You are a high school student living in the town of Charlestown, Maryland. Your house is only a few blocks from the bay. A short walk in the opposite direction takes you to a forest. A well in your backyard supplies your family with water, just as other wells provide drinking water to your Charlestown neighbors. There is no city-wide water system in Charlestown. For the past few months, some people have been complaining that their water smells funny. Dogs are refusing to drink the water and dead birds have been found near the town's spring.

Last month town commissioners asked the State Department of the Environment to test all the wells in Charlestown. The state has found that some of the wells contain dangerous levels of compounds that are commonly found in gasoline. Inspectors from the Department of the Environment think they have found that the source of contamination is a leak from one of the five underground gasoline storage tanks in town.

Fast action is needed! Your town must have clean drinking water. The rate of movement of gasoline, known as the *plume*, will be calculated by a state geologist; a method for removing the gasoline from the water will be selected by the State Department of the Environment; and a new source of water must be found by you and your classmates.

Your science teacher, who is one of the town commissioners, has volunteered your class to be the research team that will investigate the contamination and make recommendations to the commissioners and citizens of Charlestown. Your grade for this assignment—as well as your future health—will depend on the quality of your work on this project.

You will work with a group of experts. These experts include a **geologist**, an **inspector** of leaky underground storage tanks for the Maryland Department of the Environment, a professional **well driller**, an **environmental engineer** from a company that specializes in water tower supply systems, and a **gas station owner**. Useful information and recommendations on how your group would approach this task can be found in the five On the Job interviews included in this module.

For this project, your class will:

- gather information on groundwater and its movement;

- investigate the permeability and porosity of the soils on your property;

- study topographic and subsurface profiles; and

- compile other general information on wells and water supply systems.

You will use the information you gather to support a recommendation for the best place to locate a new community well. Your recommendation will be presented to the town commissioners and the residents.

You will need to create the following documents for your personal portfolio. These items will be valuable in your presentation to the town commissioners and interested citizens of Charlestown:

STUDENT VOICES

My parents had a water filter installed on our well.

I think the state should make those responsible pay for cleaning up the leak.

RICHARD MCNEILL
CHARLOTTE, NC

1. the State Department of the Environment test report on your well;
2. a prediction of the likelihood of your well becoming polluted if it is not already contaminated;
3. an explanation of the method used by the people who have contaminated wells to filter their water and make it safe for drinking;
4. a profile of the surface topography of Charlestown and the subsurface strata that shows the location of the gasoline plume;
5. a log of your family's average daily water usage; an estimate of your town's (or your class's) average daily water usage; and an estimate of monthly and yearly water usage for your town;
6. a city map with your recommended site for the new city well, with the depth clearly marked; and
7. a letter to the mayor of Charlestown explaining your reasons for selecting that site and depth. (In your letter to the mayor, you may use all data and other essential information from your portfolio to explain why your proposed well site is the best choice.)

Important Note: What you discover through your experience with this task could make you an expert in the real town where you live. You and your classmates will acquire the knowledge necessary to ask important questions—and to provide some of the answers—concerning the quality of water available in your school, your home, and your community.

Your teacher has selected this unit because you are ready to meet this challenge.

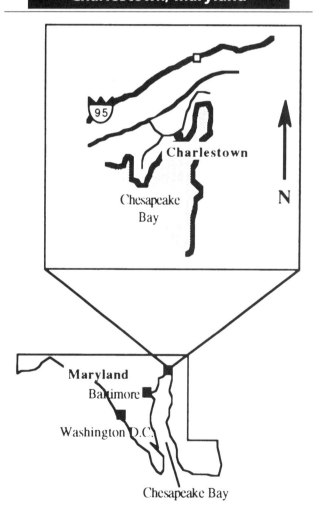

Charlestown, Maryland

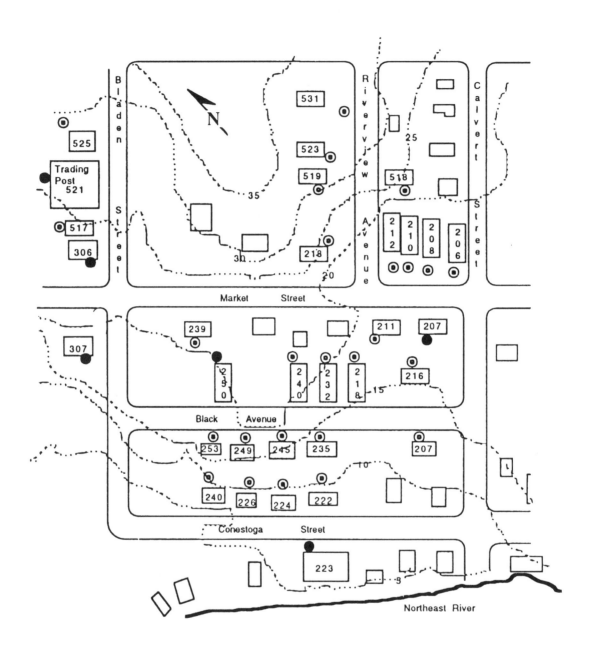

LEGEND

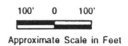 Shallow residential well (< 40 ft deep)

● Deep residential well (> 60 ft deep)

......5...... Topographic Lines (Contour interval ≈ 5')

100'   0   100'

Approximate Scale in Feet

Wells

At one time people depended solely on surface water—rivers, lakes, and streams—for their drinking water supply. People eventually discovered that in many places they could find water simply by digging a hole in the ground. They had tapped into groundwater held in aquifers.

Eventually people realized that if they lined the holes to keep the sides from caving in, they could have a clean and reliable source of water. These holes were the first shallow wells. Over the centuries, people have found different ways to make wells. The first were called *dug wells* because they were dug by hand with simple tools—a method still used today in less industrialized areas of the world.

Another type of well is called a *bored well*. It is made with a large corkscrew-shaped drill bit called an *auger*. These wells are usually shallow and lined with tiles. Today most wells are *drilled wells*. They are usually drilled by the *rotary method*, a process in which a steel bit is fastened to a pipe and rotated by a machine. As it turns, the bit pushes its way through the earth, chewing its way through the rock, until it reaches water. The hole is lined with a steel or a plastic pipe called a *casing*, which keeps the walls from caving in and protects the water from contamination.

During well construction it is important for the people drilling to dig deeply. As groundwater is removed from the well, an action called *drawdown* lowers the level of the groundwater, or *water table*. If the well is too shallow, the drawdown may cause the well to go dry even though there is still plenty of water in the aquifer.

Sometimes a well will tap into an *artesian* aquifer. In these deep wells, water is forced up by the pressure of underground water draining from higher ground. When this happens, water may gush to the surface. If this is not the case, some other source of energy must be used to bring water to the surface. A person may stand and crank a bucket up from the bottom of a well; a wind-

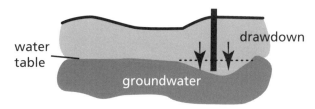

mill may use energy from the wind to replace human energy. Today the energy required is usually provided by electric motors.

Once water has been brought to the surface it may be used immediately or stored. Water towers are a common type of reservoir for water storage. Water is pumped into the tower and stored until it is needed by community homes and businesses.

Water Dowsing

How do we find water when we can't see it? Springs are the easiest place to find groundwater, but if there is no spring what can we do? Today we have advanced technology to assist us in our search for usable groundwater.

In earlier times, water dowsing—also called *water divining* or *water witching*—was used to locate underground water. Dowsers generally used a forked wooden branch from a peach, apple, or willow tree. This forked stick, or *divining rod*, was usually shaped like the letter Y. Dowsers held the forked ends of the stick in their hands with the long, single end pointed straight ahead. The dowser walked over the land, and when the rod "sensed" water underground, the single end pointed strongly to the ground. Legend tells that sometimes the rod moved so powerfully that, if the dowser was holding it very tightly, the rod could scrape the skin off the dowser's hands!

Some ancient cave paintings in northern Africa and some ancient Chinese writings suggest that water dowsers were active thousands of years ago. Although scientists have found no evidence to support the claims of water dowsing, diviners were sometimes successful in finding water in what appeared to be a dry area. Some people believe that dowsing works, others don't. Science cannot explain it yet, but many people have seen it work. What do you think?

Charlestown

Another community that found itself in a similar predicament was the quiet, little river town of Charlestown in Cecil County, Maryland. The residents' plight began in late 1986, but actually had its origins in the late 1940s. Far different from the problems spawned by a huge complex of above-ground fuel terminals, Charlestown residents had to deal with something much more common to each of us: the out-of-sight, out-of-mind danger of a leaking underground gasoline storage tank at a neighborhood gas station.

The saga of Charlestown began in October 1986, when two Charlestown residents informed Cecil County officials that their well water tasted bad. An investigation was launched by the Cecil County Health Department to identify the contamination source. Testing of the well water confirmed that quantities of benzene were present at levels higher than what is deemed "safe." The detection of benzene in the groundwater pointed to one probable cause: an underground gasoline leak. Making matters worse, in the late 1980s, most of Charlestown's population of just over 700 people depended on shallow, private wells for their water supplies. A public water supply system did not exist. Were other wells already contaminated? Would all of Charlestown's wells become contaminated too?

A majority of Charlestown's private wells were less than 30 feet deep. Of the wells that were less than 30 feet deep, most were hand-dug. Upon further investigation, health officials found as much as 3 to 4 feet of gasoline floating on top of the water in some wells.

Where was the leak coming from? Five potential sources were pinpointed. Monitoring wells were drilled near the suspected sites. Data gathered showed the Trading Post as the point of origin for the escaping petroleum. The Trading Post was a tiny convenience store and gas station, owned and operated by one family over three generations. On the property were two below-ground fuel storage tanks that supplied above-ground gasoline pumps. These tanks had been buried for about 40 years.

Unfortunately, the total amount of gasoline product that was actually leaked could not be accounted for. The reason? The operators of the Trading Post had kept sloppy records. Their records failed to show how much gasoline had been delivered to the tanks compared to the amount actually sold to customers.

In March of 1987, after the Trading Post's two underground storage systems were emptied, the tanks were dug up and inspected. Upon close examination, one tank was found to contain several holes, clearly indicating that it was the likely source for the gasoline contaminating the wells of Charlestown.

But digging up the ruptured tank did not stop the spread of gasoline already in the ground. As the petroleum crept through the underground geological maze of clay, sand, silt, and gravel it fingered outward in what is called a plume.

Heading south through Charlestown, the gasoline plume was steered by gravity, topography, capillarity, and the pumping actions of shallow wells. Moving through a shallow, upper aquifer from which most of the residents of Charlestown drew their drinking water, the carcinogenic hydrocarbons from the gasoline seeped into well after well. Some wells were polluted with the hydrocarbons above permissible limits. Many wells were found to have benzene and methyl tertiary-butyl ether (MTBE), above recommended levels.

Monitoring holes seventy-six feet deep were dug to assess the contaminating crawl of gasoline.

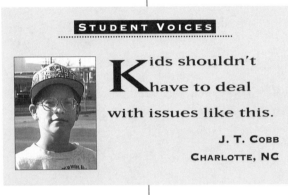

In order to remove and treat contaminated water, state-supplied pumping equipment was brought to the leak area. Almost 4,000 gallons of undissolved gasoline was removed by September 1989. The pumping lowered the area's water table.

The Maryland Department of the Environment provided free carbon filters to Charlestown residents affected by the gasoline contamination. Some townspeople refused the filters, believing that their water was not affected. Others were irritated that the government was interfering with their personal lives. In certain cases, even though measuring devices clearly indicated a fouled water supply, some residents had grown accustomed to the taste and smell of their water as it gradually changed over several years. They, too, refused the filters, believing they were not impacted by the gasoline leak.

To rid Charlestown of its problems, several actions were considered, including *bioremediation*, speeding the growth of bacteria already in the water to break down gasoline into harmless compounds. Each process had to be evaluated. The cost to implement each solution and the time required to return the quality of water to acceptable levels were the primary criteria for judging alternative solutions. Some of the suggested cleanup techniques would have taken a decade or more to fully remove the contaminants.

Cleanup takes a long time because cleaning groundwater is more difficult and costly than cleaning contaminated soil. Cleanups are expected to become even more burdensome as states tackle increasing numbers of these complicated groundwater-contamination sites.

Affected Charlestown homeowners filed two lawsuits. They sought $65 million in damages from the owners of the Trading Post. However, shortly after the investigation began, the Trading Post's owner died, leaving no heirs. In such cases, the state assumes responsibility for the cleanup while the estate is settled. The total value of the Trading Post's owner's estate did not come close to paying the cleanup bill.

Many questions were raised: Who should be responsible for paying the bill for cleanup operations? Who would reimburse homeowners for the decrease in their property values? The long-term effects of exposure to the gasoline leak on public health are still to be determined. Who will pay medical expenses if health problems are found in later years?

Several town meetings were called to help determine the best course of action to remedy the pollution problem. Today, over $1 million in cleanup costs have been passed on to the taxpayers of the entire state of Maryland. A new municipal water system, including an elevated 300,000 gallon water tank, has been installed in Charlestown. The cost for installing the new water distribution system was nearly $3 million.

Charlestown and Paw Creek are but two of the once-unsuspecting communities that came face-to-face with leaking fuel tanks. Confirmed releases of pollutants from underground storage tanks are reported nationwide at a rate of about 1,000 per week. This finding was presented to Congress in February 1993 by the U.S. Environmental Protection Agency, Office of Underground Storage Tanks, in the "Report to House Appropriations Committee on the Leaking Underground Storage Tanks Program."

How safe is your groundwater? Could there be a leaking storage tank in your neighborhood? By the time you and your classmates complete this unit, you may be the best informed "experts" in your community. Maybe your class will be called on to assist in dealing with a leaky underground storage tank in your town. ∎

IN THE NEWS

3,890 gals. of gasoline pumped; no end in sight

By Kimberly Hook
Whig Staff Writer

Since Charlestown residents began smelling and tasting gasoline in their water more than two years ago, the state has pumped 3,980 gallons of gasoline from it and there is no immediate end in sight.

After residents sought help with their problem, the state discovered that gasoline had been leaking from an underground gasoline storage tank at the Trading Postmarket for an unknown amount of time.

Robert DeMarco, chief of the state's Leaking Underground Storage Tank (LUST) removal program, said the state has spent $178,000 for contractors to remove the gasoline.

DeMarco said the state will soon put in a second system to help pump out and treat more water contaminated with undissolved gasoline. But, he said the state will wait to try to extract dissolved gasoline until the town gets a new municipal water system.

Currently, the small town of more than 800 residents is served by shallow, hand-dug or hand-driven wells of up to 15 feet. DeMarco said the state cannot extract the dissolved gasoline without the risk of drying up the town's shallow wells.

The state is paying for the cleanup, but will seek to recover costs from those responsible for the tanks, DeMarco said.

Originally, the state considered Postmarket owner Judy B. Deller of Perryville and Francis D. L. Graham, who owns the lands on which the market and the tanks were located, plus Alger Inc., responsible for the cleanup. Alger has always denied owning the leaking tanks. Deller and Graham agreed to have them removed and replaced.

CECIL WHIG, SEPTEMBER 27, 1989

Wicked Wicking

Purpose
To describe and demonstrate capillary action.

Background
It's vacation time and your family is going camping! Your mom is worried that the house plants will die while you're away, so she uses a pencil to poke a hole in the soil of each plant. Then she takes long lengths of cotton string and buries one end of the string in each hole. She neatly braids the strings together and places the braided strings in a one-gallon milk jug filled with water.

But wait a minute! The jug is on a shelf lower than the plants. How can the plants get the water they need? Water cannot flow uphill! You want to bet your mom ten dollars that the plants will dry out and die while you're gone. But you've worked hard for your money. You decide to do an experiment to find out whether or not to bet. In your experiment you will also find out what this has to do with groundwater and the leaking gasoline under your town.

Materials (depending on the procedure used)

For each pair:
- One paper or plastic cup
- A piece of thin cotton string, 40 centimeters long
- Ring stand and ring
- Two 1- or 2-liter clear plastic bottles, empty
- One 1- or 2-liter clear plastic bottle, filled with water
- Large, wide bowl
- Large funnel
- Nail or awl

For the class:
- Food coloring
- Paper towels
- Fine sand
- Coarse sand
- Stop watch or wall clock with second hand
- Water

Procedure A
1. Set up a ring stand and ring. Tie the piece of string to the ring. Place a cup so that the free end of the string is touching the bottom of the cup.
2. Put several milliliters of food coloring (or a dark mixture of food coloring and water) in the cup. Position the cup so that the string touches the food coloring.
3. Record your observations.
4. Brainstorm a list of practical applications for the phenomenon you just observed.

Procedure B
1. Poke several holes in the bottom of a plastic bottle. Place the bottle in a bowl. Fill the bottle half way with fine sand, but make sure the holes stay open.
2. Pour water into the bowl until it surrounds the bottle and sand. Observe the sand in the bottle. Watch the water level carefully and record your observations.
3. Repeat steps one and two using coarse sand.
4. (Optional) Use various combinations of the two types of sands. Try placing a layer of clay between the two layers of sand.

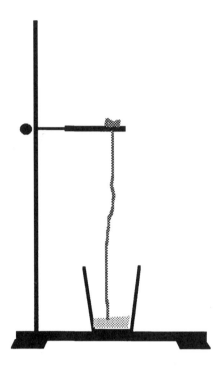

Questions
1. Will you bet your mom? Why or why not?
2. What happened to the string?
3. Which type of sand absorbed water most rapidly?
4. Did the water rise higher in the bottle with fine sand or in the bottle with coarse sand?
5. How does groundwater move uphill?

Conclusion
Write a short, two-character dialogue or play where you are talking to your five-year-old brother or sister who has five dollars and wants to be a part of the bet. In the dialogue be sure to explain your reasons for thinking that the bet is a good idea or one that is unwise. Make sure your words are ones that a five-year-old can understand.

Septic Systems

The septic system for sewage treatment is generally used for a single dwelling or apartment that is too far away to be connected to a city sewage treatment system. In 1990, the U.S. Environmental Protection Agency reported that approximately one-fourth of all homes in the U.S. rely on septic systems to dispose of their human wastes.

A septic system usually consists of: (1) an underground tank where solids can settle to the bottom to be broken down by bacteria; and (2) a leach bed, which distributes liquid from the tank over a large area of subsurface soil.

When deciding where to place the leach field, installers first conduct a percolation test. For the system to work properly, the soil has to have an adequate rate of *percolation*, the measure of how fast the water is absorbed by the soil in the proposed leach field area.

The Percolation Test

Percolation test holes are dug at either end of the proposed area for the ground absorption field. A minimum of two holes are dug, 12 inches in diameter, or 12 inches square, to the depth of the proposed disposal field, usually 22 to 32 inches deep. The holes are pre-soaked, or saturated, by filling them with water and keeping them filled for four hours.

After saturation, the holes are filled to the top immediately with water, the water is allowed to drain within five inches of the bottom of the hole, and then this step is repeated. Water is added to bring the level to six inches from the bottom, then observers time how long it takes for the level to drop one inch.

The time is recorded. This procedure is repeated until the last two rates of fall do not vary by more than two minutes. All the times are recorded. The percolation rate is determined by averaging the slowest rates recorded for each percolation test hole in minutes per inch. The holes are then covered and their locations flagged for inspection.

Ideally, wastewater is filtered by the soil before it reaches the groundwater. The sludge in the tank is pumped out about once every five years. Septic systems are economical and easy to use, but when there are too many septic tanks in a small area, the soil loses its ability to purify the wastewater before it reaches the water table.

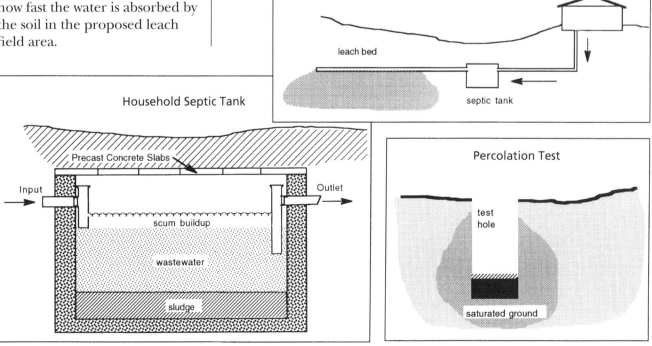

A Typical Septic System

leach bed

septic tank

Household Septic Tank

Precast Concrete Slabs

Input

Outlet

scum buildup

wastewater

sludge

Percolation Test

test hole

saturated ground

A City and Its Water

Throughout history, people have settled near sources of water. Nomads of prehistoric times wandered from place to place, stopping where they found good watering holes and green pastures. Ancient civilizations of Egypt, Mesopotamia, India, and China grew up along riverbanks. Today people still settle close enough to water to enjoy its benefits, while staying far enough from the water's edge to avoid floods.

Notice the location of cities in our own country. Usually, they are close to a river, a lake, or have access to sufficient groundwater. When rivers are unreliable or are insufficient to supply a growing population, people often build dams, ensuring a permanent water supply. If no convenient water source exists, people can send water long distances through pipelines, ditches, or aqueducts and store it in reservoirs.

Technology today has allowed us to provide large amounts of water to people who live far from a source of water. Water shortages, however, are an ever-present danger for any country. We are all dependent on often unpredictable weather patterns, whether we live near to or far from a water source. During drought years in arid regions such as Southern California, water is often rationed.

The City Water Supply

Cities acquire water either from nearby surface water or groundwater sources. As you probably know, we cannot assume that water in rivers, lakes, and below ground is safe to drink. A city's water supply must first be purified at a water-treatment facility, often called the *waterworks*, to render it safe and drinkable.

At most water-treatment plants, water passes through coarse screens at the source to remove silt, sewage, or large objects. Then the water enters a mixing tank where chemical coagulants are added to help separate out impurities. Coagulants cause particles in the water to clump together and become dense enough to sink. Coagulants combine with bacteria, mud, and silt to form jelly-like globs called *flocs*. Other things added to the water include chlorine to kill harmful organisms, a copper compound to destroy microscopic plant life, and other chemicals that help remove any bad taste or smell.

After going through the mixing tank, the water flows into deep, wide sedimentation tanks where the flocs settle to the bottom. Then the water makes its way to the filtering system where sand, gravel, or hard coal strain the water and remove bacteria and other suspended waste. More chlorine is added to keep bacteria from developing as the water travels to your house. Many cities also add fluoride to their water to help prevent tooth decay.

In some communities, water leaving the waterworks is especially *hard*— it contains minerals that make it difficult for soap to lather. In locations where hard water is a problem, the waterworks may add soda ash or lime to "soften" the water. Some people will install water-softening systems in their homes if their water is hard.

Who pays for the expensive processing of all this water? In the past, cities taxed property owners for water use. Today, most cities require businesses and homes to have water meters, which measure exactly how much water is used and allow the city to charge accordingly. How does your community pay for its water?

How does this clean water get to your house? Water leaves the waterworks in large underground pipes called *water mains*. These take the water to all parts of your community. These mains also take water directly to fire hydrants. Large water main pipes are made of cast iron, coated steel, or concrete. Smaller pipes, often made of copper, carry water from the large mains to consumers.

Something must force the water into your pipes and out your faucet. In mountainous areas, water might be stored high above the town so that gravity can provide enough pressure to carry water to consumers. In small towns, water might be stored in a tank on a hilltop or in a large tower. If you have traveled through rural areas, you may have seen these water towers or tanks. Many of them bear the name of the town for which they supply water. This is now the case in Charlestown, Maryland.

When water is released into the mains, the water flows downward, assisted by the pull of gravity. Pressure is provided by the water that remains in the tank or tower. Usually, though, city water departments must use pumps to push the water through the mains and into the homes of its customers. The average city dweller in our country uses, either directly or indirectly, about 150 gallons of water a day. This total includes each individual's share of the water used for community needs like fire fighting, waste disposal, and industry.

Once water reaches your home it is ready for drinking.

But some people still aren't happy. They prefer to use home water-treatment units to treat their "tap" water. Several types of these units are available. A basic filter only removes the suspended solids and chemicals that add taste and odor. An additional charcoal filter removes certain organic compounds (those that contain chlorine and bromine) as well as some organic pollutants. Other processes available to homes with serious water-purification needs include distilling and disinfecting. You and your class may want to discuss and then try out a few different methods for cleaning water.

MDE investigation to delay Charlestown wells for a year

by Stuart Hirsch
Whig Annapolis Correspondent
ANNAPOLIS--Construction of Charlestown's new drinking wells will be delayed at least one year while the Department of Environment investigates the extent of groundwater contamination from an abandoned landfill near the proposed well sites.

The state Board of Public Works yesterday approved a $300,000 grant to study contamination from the Louisa Lane dump, which was used during the 1960's and closed in 1972.

Initial data from tests performed last June shows the presence of low levels of lead and chromium at the old dump site, which is located about 3,800 feet from the planned Charlestown wells, said John Goheen, a spokesman for the Maryland Department of Environment.

Town officials were set to begin construction of the new water system when trace levels of the pollutants were first discovered last fall, said Eric Johnston, Charlestown's town administrator.

Now, Johnston said, "we're hoping that the project will be far enough along so we can receive funding this fall and construction can begin in the spring (of 1991)."

A new municipal water system was already in the planning stages when a leaking underground storage tank was found to be contaminating some shallow wells of town residents, said David Jarinko, a town board member.

That discovery only made completion of the $3 million water project more urgent.

"It's always better to err on the side of caution when you're dealing with a public health issue...But this delay is disappointing and frustrating," Jarinko said.

The Cecil County project was one of three such groundwater contamination investigations approved by the Board of Public Works Wednesday.

Money for the projects, $1.55 million in all, will come from the state's Controlled Hazardous Substance Cleanup Loan of 1988.

CECIL WHIG, APRIL 12, 1990

Spaces in Places

Purpose

To measure the space between sediment particles and the rate of water flow through the particles.

Materials

- Sand
- Clay
- Potting soil
- Two 100-ml beakers (or two clear plastic cups)
- A 100-ml graduated cylinder
- Coffee filters
- Masking tape
- Rubber bands
- Scissors
- Stop watch or wall clock with second hand

Background

Several homeowners in Charlestown have been told that their wells are contaminated with gasoline. Others have been told that, because they have deep wells, and because a layer of clay protects the deeper water, their water is safe to drink. Most people with deep wells don't believe their water is really safe.

You are a science student who has been studying the contamination issue. You and your partner have been asked to come to a town meeting to explain porosity and permeability to these skeptical homeowners and to demonstrate how the clay layer is able to protect their water. While looking through your notes, you found diagrams of an experiment on porosity and permeability. You decide to use the materials shown in the diagrams to develop demonstrations that will help with your presentation. But first, you want to

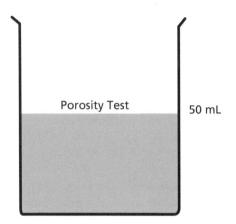

Porosity Test   50 mL

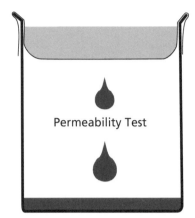

Permeability Test

try out the setups, modifying them as necessary, to test the permeability and porosity of sand, clay, and potting soil, and to develop a display of the resulting data.

Definitions

Porosity is a measure of the amount of space between particles. The more porous a material, the more space there is between its particles. To measure porosity, simply measure the amount of water it takes to completely fill the spaces in a given volume of material. In your demonstration you must be able to show the difference in porosity of sand, potting soil, and clay. Remember, porosity is expressed as a percentage.

Permeability is a measure of the speed with which a liquid or a gas diffuses through a substance. The faster the liquid passes through a substance, the greater the permeability of that substance. In your demonstration you must be able to show the permeability of sand, potting soil, and clay. Express the permeability of each substance in liters per minute.

Think about these questions and test them as you prepare setups.

1. Will tapping the container cause the material to settle? Does this increase or decrease the porosity? Does this increase or decrease the permeability?
2. How does the shape of the grains affect porosity and permeability?
3. How does the sediment grain size affect porosity and permeability?

Conclusion

One or two teams will be selected at random to make a presentation to the entire town (class). Be prepared to perform your demonstration! Keep your data as part of your portfolio.

Size of sediment particles	
Median diameter in millimeters	Name of particle
256–129	boulder
128–65	cobble
64–2.1	gravel
2.0–0.126	sand
0.125–0.008	silt
0.004 or smaller	clay

Earth: The Water Planet

Water, water, everywhere? Not when you're considering the entire solar system in which Earth resides. The planets in our solar system are divided into two groups: the "terrestrial" planets—Mercury, Venus, Earth, and Mars—and the "gaseous" planets—Jupiter, Saturn, Uranus, and Neptune. Lonely Pluto, usually the outermost world, is thought by some to be an escaped moon of Neptune. (Pluto's classification as either a "gaseous" or "terrestrial" planet has not yet been determined.) Contrasting Earth with the other planets is called comparative planetology.

Earth is literally awash with water. Our neighboring terrestrial planets, Venus and Mars, have very little water. Sun-parched Mercury is now believed to retain only small quantities of water as well.

Venus, Earth, and Mars all have atmospheres with clouds that interact with the warmth of the Sun. But the clouds' makeup is markedly different among the three planets. Clouds on Earth are comprised primarily of water. On Venus, clouds are made of sulfuric acid. The clouds on dry Mars are mostly dust.

There is some evidence to suggest that Venus may once have held an amount of water similar to the amount of water now present on Earth. However, the current carbon dioxide–rich atmosphere on Venus has created a runaway greenhouse effect. This has resulted in the hot, dry surface of Venus today. Venus has a dull red surface and is surrounded by a carbon dioxide–laden atmosphere 90 times thicker than ours.

Mars, on the other hand, appears to have had a denser, warmer, and more moist atmosphere in its past. In fact, large features that look like river-beds cut across the planet, suggesting that at one time Mars had considerable amounts of flowing water. We don't know what happened to this water.

Being 70 percent covered with water, Earth is unique in the solar system. How did water come to appear on our planet? One commonly held belief is that shortly after its formation, Earth's surface had thousands of active volcanoes that spewed gases into the sky for millions of years. These expelled gases contained water molecules carried from deep within the earth. Then the earth cooled gradually, and a thick atmosphere with clouds of water vapor formed. Rain falling from these clouds began to collect into what we now know as the oceans. Basically, this theory holds that the water came from within Earth itself.

Another theory, considered more speculative than the one described above, holds that a steady bombardment of comets over a long amount of time acted as water carriers, providing Earth with its reservoir of water. Telescopes on Earth and robotic probes sent into space have found, however, that comets are large clumps of dust, frozen water, and gases.

Even if we do not agree on the theory of water's origin, we all agree that water is vital to all life on Earth.

Inspector

NORVIE EMMANUEL
MARYLAND DEPARTMENT OF
THE ENVIRONMENT
BALTIMORE, MD

I am a regional inspector for the Maryland Department of the Environment. My job is to inspect gas stations, and to respond to gas and oil spills wherever they happen.

Our department works closely with all the fire departments in Maryland and with a group called Emergency Response. We are on call around-the-clock, 24 hours a day. If a spill or leak is reported in the middle of the night, we're there.

A good inspector needs to know how to deal with the public, how to be a good observer, and how to follow EPA procedures when collecting water and soil samples. A good inspector also needs a sense of curiosity.

A typical day for me can involve meeting on-site with gasoline suppliers (I oversee them as they remove a storage tank or upgrade a gas station), responding to a spill or other emergency, overseeing the installation of groundwater monitoring wells, or meeting with citizens who are having problems that relate to gasoline or oil.

People sometimes become irate when I tell them that we suspect a leak coming from their tank and that they must remove the tank or fill it with a slurry to abandon it properly. They are irate because it can cost a lot of money if a cleanup is involved. But groundwater is very precious and needs to be protected. It's my job to make sure that gasoline and oil don't pollute it.

Many citizens are not aware of how much damage oil and gas cause to our groundwater. They resent the state requiring them to clean up a leak. We listen to them and are as understanding as possible, but we urge them to remove a leaking tank right away. The longer the leak continues, the more costly the cleanup will be. And if their neighbors' wells are polluted, that is a serious health problem. I try to prevent that.

Gas stations are now required by law to use tanks and pipes that are designed to prevent or catch leaks. Underground tanks made of bare steel have to be replaced by 1998, but many stations are already making the change. That's keeping us quite busy. Steel tanks must be replaced with tanks that are able to withstand the corrosive effects of electricity in the ground.

In college, I majored in nursing and the life sciences. I took classes in general math, college algebra, statistics, zoology, chemistry, and botany, so I had a good background for an environmental sciences job. The chemistry and biology I learned in high school and college is essential to my work. I use math and science every day.

I do a lot of reading and studying to keep up with my job. I read the latest reports from the Environmental Protection Agency (EPA), and I attend classes on new technologies. I try to take as many courses as I can.

When we visited the site of the gasoline leak in Charlestown, there was a strong smell of gasoline coming from the water. I was amazed that people were actually drinking it. My first concern was to warn the people not to drink their water until I could arrange to have a water-treatment system installed. I was very concerned about their health.

After the water-treatment systems were installed, another odor became apparent. It smelled like hard-boiled eggs. After testing for a number of pollutants, we discovered hydrogen sulfide coming from decaying *E. coli* bacteria in the soil. *E. coli* is present in human feces. It probably came from old outhouses that were abandoned many years ago. The *E. coli* didn't appear to affect the residents of Charlestown.

Before the water system was installed in Charlestown, the town's well water always had an orange hue to it from the presence of iron. White clothes took on an orange color from being washed in it. Blue and green rings in sinks and bathtubs indicated that other metals were present too. We tested and found trace amounts of chromium.

Many interesting careers in environmental sciences don't require masters or doctorate degrees. With a couple of years of college education, a person can move into challenging jobs like mine. It's not too late for you to become one of the pioneers in this field. I love this job!

Well Driller

WILLIAM JEFFERYS
A.C. SCHULTES, INC.
EDGEWATER, MD

I'm the president of A. C. Schultes, Inc. Our 110 employees make us one of the largest well-drilling companies in the mid-Atlantic region. My days are spent in the office or on the road, where I am seeing customers and bidding on new work. I really miss doing the field work: drilling wells, investigating the geology and hydrology of an area, doing the detective work. That's the real fun of my job.

My father just retired after 45 years with the company. When I was a boy, he took me to work with him. We built water systems and pumping stations, and we drilled water wells. In 1980, when I became a project manager and administrator for the company, it felt funny telling my father what to do.

My college degree is in geology, but I took courses in biology and chemistry, too. The calculus and math I took help me calculate volumes and pressures. I use science and math every day.

We don't just drill for water, we do all kinds of environmental drilling. When there's a spill we drill wells to monitor the groundwater. We drill recovery wells to pump out the toxic material we find. It takes special training to handle hazardous waste and to understand proper protection for your workers.

Our work on the water system for Charlestown began with a test well to determine the amount of water available at the site. Certain places we drilled had no water at all. So we drilled a lot of holes to find the best sites for the production wells. Charlestown is a rough area to drill in. There's a lot of water, a lot of clay, but not a lot of sand. You find water in sand, not clay.

A household of four needs about 250 gallons of water a day. We normally design a system that can supply three times that average. That means we plan for 750 gallons of water per family, per day, to cover peak water use. We then decide how much storage we're going to need, and how many wells it will take to replenish the water.

Wells are a good source of water. Groundwater has a lot of advantages over lakes and rivers. It has a constant temperature, and it is better protected from contamination.

Drilling wells can be very interesting. Sometimes when we drill, we come up with some strange things. In southern Maryland for example, there is an underground formation called the Aquia. It's famous because it has a lot of shells and fossils in it.

Drilling for water is dangerous, too. Groundwater is a natural conductor of electricity, so you have to be very careful not to hit buried electrical cables.

Gas Station Dealer-Manager

JOHN DISTAD
AMOCO
WASHINGTON, D.C.

I'm the dealer and manager of the Washington, D.C., Amoco station that my father opened in 1959. I've been working at the station since I was about your age. But before Amoco would take me on as the station's dealer, I had to go to Chicago for a two-week dealer's training course. They taught me how to manage the business. The training included basic record keeping. Of course you have to be able to read and write in English, and have a good understanding of math before you ever start. Amoco also checks to make sure you have enough backing (money) to run the operation correctly.

Good record keeping is vital if you are going to detect a leak before it does too much damage. The government requires us to keep good records. Amoco requires a daily inventory check to catch leaks.

Every morning we manually measure the gas in our underground tanks using a long measuring stick. At the end of the day we read the pumps and then subtract our total sales from the morning's tank readings. The next morning when we "stick" (measure) the tanks again, we compare the new measurement with yesterday's calculations to be sure we haven't lost any gasoline. If we started with 10,000 gallons and we sold 6,000 there should be 4,000 gallons left.

We also have a computer that monitors our tanks and pumps. It automatically checks the amount of gasoline. We compare the computer's numbers with the numbers that we calculate when we manually look for errors and leaks.

Checking both manually and by computer is important for another reason. If the power goes out, the computer goes out, too. At least we will have the manual measurements. Power failures don't happen very often in the city, but in rural areas they happen all the time.

One of the things we consider when figuring our daily totals is the temperature. When gasoline is in the ground, it's stays at about 55 degrees year-round. But when gasoline is trucked to the gas station in the summer, it gets hot and expands, and in the winter it gets cold and contracts. So the measurements can vary a little depending on the season and whether or not the gas was just delivered. When you're talking about 10,000 gallons, this expansion and contraction causes measurements to vary a few gallons even when there is no leak.

Of course the main thing we're worried about is shortages. Daily monitoring will pick up a leak quickly. If we have a hole in our tank or a line that is broken or leaking, we could lose a lot of gas over a few days. So far, we haven't had that problem at my station.

If Amoco thinks one of their stations has a leak, they send someone to test the gas lines and tanks. Most companies also test the lines and tanks once a year whether they need to or not. The accuracy of the pumps is also checked by the companies and the state to make sure the customer is getting the amount of gas they pay for.

At my station we have four underground storage tanks. Each one holds 10,000 gallons. Around the tanks are water-monitoring wells that are checked regularly for any evidence of gasoline in the groundwater. Since my station is near the subway, the transit authority installed about a dozen wells around our tanks. If gasoline leaked into the subway tunnels, it could cause serious problems.

We also have rods in the ground around the station that measure *electrolysis*. Electrolysis is electrical activity that can corrode metal in the tanks and pipes. Once a year we take readings of the electrical energy in the soil to help us predict how long our tanks will last.

After about 15 years, new tanks will be installed to replace the old tanks.

You may not realize it, but when somebody spills gasoline, it doesn't all evaporate. Some of it soaks through the concrete and down into the soil. Over the years, we have had some contamination that was traced to spillage. Special equipment was used to pump the contaminated groundwater through a filtering system that separates the gasoline from the water. The water was put into the sewage system, and the recovered gasoline was hauled off as hazardous waste.

If an oil company owns the tanks, it pays for the cleanup when gasoline or oil leaks. Whoever owns the tanks pays the bill. In the past, some oil companies gave tanks away to gas station dealers so that the dealers would be legally responsible if a leak developed. Amoco doesn't do that. As long as I report a leak as soon as I know about it, Amoco will take responsibility for the problem.

If you have more questions about these issues, call your favorite oil company. Most oil companies will be happy to answer your questions. Community relations is a high priority to them.

Charlestown residents file $65 million suit

By David Healey
Whig Staff Writer

Lawsuit claims companies at fault for gasoline leakage in well water

Two lawsuits seeking some $65 million in damages have been filed against the parties allegedly responsible for contaminating some Charlestown wells with gasoline.

Gasoline-contaminated wells have troubled Charlestown residents for several years. A state survey in 1987 determined that as much as 3 to 4 feet of gasoline was floating on top of the water in some wells. At that time, state officials said 30 wells contained some gasoline, and nearly half of those wells had gasoline levels that made the well water unsafe to drink. The gasoline leaked from underground storage tanks at the Trading Postmarket, a small store and gas station in Charlestown, state officials said.

The two suits were filed March 8 in Cecil County Circuit Court by present and former tenants at 510 Riverview Avenue. They are respresented by Leight D. Collins, an attorney for the Baltimore law firm of Pfeifer & Fabian. Named as defendants in the case are Alger Oil Inc. in Port Deposit; Getty Oil Company; Judy B. Deller, owner of the Trading Postmarket and Francis D. L. Graham of Charlestown, who leases his property to Deller.

Seven plaintiffs

A total of seven plaintiffs are named in the separate lawsuits, many of them children from the Stiltner Stroupe families. The Stiltners lived at 510 Riverview from 1972 until March 1984, when they moved to a new home on Market Street in Charlestown. The Stroupes have lived at the property since 1984. Both the Market Street and Riverview property is owned by Mary Stroupe Marshall of Charlestown, the suit said.

The suit filed last week claimed that Alger and Getty, as owners of the gasoline pumps, piping and storage tanks at the Trading Postmarket, were negligent in failing to stop the leaking tanks.

"Although Defendants knew or should have known of the leakage, Defendants failed to replace the underground tanks and/or other equipment located on Defendants land or take action to halt the leakage," the suit said.

Filter system installed

The suit contended that once the defendants' wells were contaminated with the carcinogenic hydrocarbons from the gasoline, the well water could no longer be used.

According to state officials, Maryland spent approximately $18,000 in 1987 to install a carbon filtration system in neighborhood wells to remove some of the gasoline and make the water drinkable.

The suit further claimed the defendants made no attempt to correct the groundwater contamination despite the alleged severe mental, emotional and physical distress and possible health problems caused by the gasoline-tainted water.

Consequently, the plaintiffs are seeking compensation as well as "punitive damages" for a total of 20 counts in the two lawsuits. The lawsuits seek damages for negligence, potential health problems and other claims. Judy B. (Deller) Newsome, owner of the Trading Postmaket, said Tuesday she would rather not comment on the lawsuit.

Attempts to reach managers of Alger Oil and Getty Oil proved unsuccessful. However, a spokesman for Getty's resident agent, Prentice Hall Corporation Systems in Baltimore, confirmed that the lawsuit had been served on Getty.

Charlestown is in the process of installing a town water and sewage system. Homeowners' shallow wells have often been affected by drought and sewage contamination, officials said.

CECIL WHIG, MARCH 14, 1990

Above and Below

Purpose

To investigate surface topography and subsurface soil layers.

Background

You and the other residents of Charlestown are having a difficult time believing your water supply is polluted by a leaking gasoline storage tank at the Trading Post. Some wells that are downhill from the Trading Post are contaminated and others are not.

A geologist has explained to the residents that there are two aquifers under Charlestown. Some people draw water from a shallow aquifer while others draw their water from a deep aquifer. You and your neighbors are skeptical, so you asked to see evidence. A well-drilling company conducted tests by digging seventy-six-foot deep test holes and now the company's representative has provided each of Charlestown's homeowners with a report explaining the results of their tests. These reports identify the types of sediment and their depths under each property.

You and your science teacher have decided to construct a profile showing a cross section of the town. The cross section will show layers of sediment, or *strata*, from the surface down to where the water is located in a deep aquifer.

The mayor needs a letter and a copy of your work, so do the best job you can.

Materials

- Official Drilling Logs, to be provided by your teacher
- Charlestown map with a line (provided by your teacher)
- A strip of adding machine paper
- Graph paper
- Pencil
- Tracing paper
- Colored pencils
- Pens for highlighting
- Ruler
- Tape

Procedure

1. Locate and circle your house on the town map. Then circle the leaking gasoline tank at the Trading Post located at 521 Bladen Street and circle the arrow that indicates north.
2. Locate the line running from Point A to Point B. This line, Line AB, is called the profile line. Highlight the profile line. Study the Discovery File "Constructing a Topographic Profile," page 27.
3. Use the profile line and a sheet of graph paper to construct the surface profile.
4. Use drilling log reports and a strip of adding machine paper to construct a subsurface profile of your property. Use the scale 1 inch = 2 feet. Add a vertical line to show your well, and draw a picture of your house at the top of the adding machine strip. Label your house with your name and address.
5. Everyone whose house lies on, or is close to, Line AB should help construct an enlarged copy of their surface profile on the blackboard or along a wall of your classroom. Use the scale 1 inch = 20 feet for

horizontal measurements and 1 inch = 2 feet for vertical measurements.

6. Those same people whose houses lie on or close to Line AB should now tape their subsurface profiles on the large copy of the surface profile that has been placed along the wall. They will connect "like" layers between neighbors subsurface profiles and key them appropriately. Make sure the spacing between houses is accurate based on the scale you are using.

7. Everyone should add the subsurface strata to their surface profiles and shade them to show the different layers.

Conclusion

Your class has been asked by the mayor to make a copy of the town profile. The mayor will select the best profile to use at the next meeting of the town commissioners. The mayor also needs answers to the following questions:

1. Are the layers uniform in thickness?

2. Do all of the houses located over the gasoline plume have contaminated wells? Why or why not?

3. From the data you have seen so far, can you determine whether the two sand layers are connected? Explain.

4. Do you think the gasoline plume will grow? If so, predict the direction in which it is most likely to grow.

Now write a letter to the mayor in which you answer the questions and offer to come to the town meeting to explain what you and your class have found.

Constructing a Topographic Profile

1. Lay a strip of paper across a topographic map. Make sure the strip lies beside the line you wish to profile.
2. Mark the paper strip where each contour line contacts the edge of the strip. (See the top figure.)
3. Label each mark with the elevation indicated on the contour line.
4. Now transfer the marks on the strip to a graph with horizontal lines. (See the bottom figure.)
5. Connect all points with a smooth line.

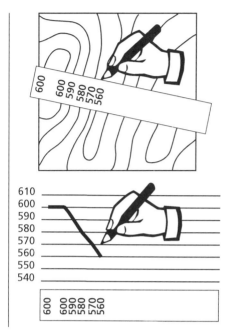

Our drinking water was brown and smelled like gasoline, and we smelled gasoline in the air. We had to get drinking water from my grandparents' house, about one mile away. We also had to do our laundry away from home.

We want a large house, but we can't sell our house in Paw Creek because of the contamination.

My friend's mother lost a baby because of the gas fumes. My neighbors, Mr. and Mrs. Killman, had their property bought by Amoco. Mrs. Killman died of cancer, Mr. Killman has leukemia, and his daughter has cancer. This scares me. I'm afraid I'll die.

LAURA LOVE
PAW CREEK, NC

Geologist

BARBARA BROWN
MARYLAND DEPARTMENT OF
THE ENVIRONMENT
BALTIMORE, MD

It's ironic—I trained to be an oil-company geologist, but today I work for the Maryland Department of the Environment. Half of my time is spent investigating sites where gasoline or fuel oil has leaked from underground storage tanks. I have been closely involved with the investigation and cleanup of Charlestown's leaky underground gasoline tank.

A fascinating thing about being a geologist in the environmental business is that geology is so much a part of everything else. I don't spend my days looking at rocks. My work involves chemistry, biology, physics, engineering, hydrology—even toxicology. Everybody wants to know how the chemicals that are leaking into the groundwater or the soil will affect people, animals, and plants. If you know that grass reacts to gasoline in a certain way, you can look for signs of leakage in the grass itself. A background in chemistry allows you to know how chemicals interact with water. The knowledge that I acquired in all of the science classes that I took in middle school, in high school, and in college, has been essential to my every day work.

Just like all scientists, I am a detective. To understand how far the leak in Charlestown had traveled and how to plan for the

cleanup, we had to understand which way the groundwater flows, and how the rocks and soil and all the hydrologic processes work together.

I like meeting the public and answering their questions. When people find chemicals in their water, they are scared. They worry about their property values and their health. So, in addition to handling the problem itself, I explain what's happening and tell people how they can help to correct the problem. Sometimes I have to advise citizens of their responsibilities under state law, deal with construction contractors, and educate public officials and the media. It's an exciting job. Each day is different.

Every time I get involved in laboratory work—collecting samples and dealing with people in the lab—I remember my laboratory classes in school. Sometimes they were boring, lots of going-by-the-book and step-by-step procedures. However, in a real laboratory, quality control is very important. Analyzing drinking water and other samples requires checking and double-checking.

A new cleanup technique, called *bioremediation*, makes use of some of Earth's tiniest living organisms. Bacteria, fungi, and other microbes in the soil actually eat up the oil or gas in contaminated soil or water. When microbes get a "slug" of food, they need oxygen to break it down. But once the oxygen is gone, they stop eating. A lot of bioremediation is not about adding "bugs" to the ground, it's about getting oxygen to the "bugs" already there.

A geologist looks at the present to help interpret the past. If you look at what's going on today, you see rivers eroding away mountains and depositing the mountains' minerals downstream. Look at a stream and you'll see gravel bars and sandbars. In areas where the water is quiet, you will find silt. This process went on in the past, too. The Appalachian Mountains were once as tall as the Rocky Mountains. A lot of sediment eroded off those mountains.

But that's the big picture. As a geologist, I also study how layers of soil are formed. For instance, to understand how layers of sand and clay are deposited, you can shake up dirt and water in a jar. Big clumps, like sand, fall to the bottom first. The water stays muddy and hazy for a long period of time, as the very fine particles that form the layers of clay settle out.

One nice thing about being a geologist is that you get dirty. So if you're the type of person who doesn't want to sit in an office and who likes to get dirt under your fingernails occasionally, this can be an exciting field.

Soil Formation

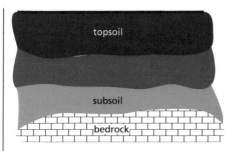

You probably think of the earth beneath your feet as just dirt—pretty much the same wherever you go. Pedologists, scientists who study dirt (they prefer to call it soil), have found that soil is actually pretty unique.

Soil is created from rock by a process called *weathering*. Weathering breaks rock into particles ranging in size from the smallest fine clays, through the medium-sized particles called *silt*, the larger particles of course sand, and up to small stones known as *gravel*. Water and air move easily through the gaps and spaces between the larger particles. They move very slowly through the tiny spaces between the smallest clay particles.

Chemical changes in the soil help bacteria, fungi, and plants to grow. Plant roots help to hold the particles of soil together; fallen leaves protect the soil from erosion when it rains; as earthworms burrow through the soil, they create air passages and lift minerals up from the depths, only to replace those minerals with decaying organic matter from the surface.

Living and decaying plants provide food for burrowing insects, worms, and larger creatures. Animal droppings and dead plants and animals are decomposed by bacteria and fungi and converted into a dark, fertile, partially decomposed material called *humus*. The main components of soil are inorganic (air, water, and minerals) and organic (living organisms, decaying dead organisms, and humus).

If you could cut a slice down through the soil where you live, you would see layers called *horizons*. The first layer—*topsoil*—is usually dark and rich in humus, as just described. The next horizon is rich in minerals and organic substances washed down from the topsoil, but is paler in color, more compact, and less fertile. Below is the subsoil that consists of infertile particles weathered from the bedrock beneath it.

Bedrock, or parent rock, is largely responsible for a soil's texture. Soil type is influenced mainly by climate, but also by topography, time, and vegetation. Soil depth can range from less than 2.5 centimeters (about 1 inch) on steep slopes to several meters on plains. (A meter is a little more than a yard.)

Over time, soil in one area may be washed away only to be deposited in another area. If deposition of soil continues over thousands of years, very thick deposits can form. These deposits can eventually turn into a kind of rock called *sedimentary rock*.

The Water Cycle

Water is constantly on the move. The rain that falls on rooftops, on the ground, and on pavement eventually flows into streams. Streams flow into rivers, and rivers flow into the ocean. Gigantic rivers of ice called glaciers are moving, too, though at a very slow pace.

Water is continually changing its form as it passes through an immense, ever-moving cycle. The sun heats the water on the surface of Earth, converting it into water vapor in the atmosphere. As the water vapor rises, it cools and begins to condense around specks of dust and crystals of salt to form tiny droplets. These droplets form clouds and eventually fall back to Earth in the form of rain, sleet, snow, and hail.

Much of this precipitation falls into the sea. As for the droplets that fall on land, they either evaporate, soak into the ground, or slowly return to the sea by way of streams and rivers. When the water droplets reach the sea, the cycle begins again.

This cycle temporarily cleans the world's water. When water evaporates from the surface of the oceans, rivers, lakes, or even parking lots, it is totally free of pollutants. However, as water falls to Earth, it begins to become recontaminated. First it picks up pollutants from the atmosphere. Then, as it flows over and under the ground and into rivers and seas, it picks up dissolved minerals and the chemical pollutants we have spread on the soil through agriculture and industry.

The contaminated water reaches the sea, and begins the cycle again by evaporating. It rises as clean water vapor to form clouds, leaving impurities behind. But with every turn of the cycle, more pollutants are carried into lakes and oceans, and the biological, chemical, and physical processes that break down these pollutants get further and further behind. What do you think happens then?

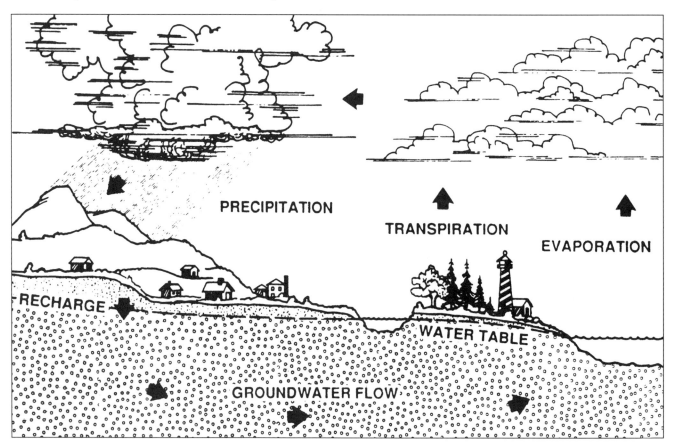

Environmental Engineer

PETER D'ADAMO
TATMAN AND LEE
ASSOCIATES
WILMINGTON, DE

My company designs and installs water and waste-water systems for a variety of clients. When Charlestown discovered a leaking gasoline tank in the center of town, we were hired to design and build a new community water-supply system. On projects like Charlestown's, I manage everything: planning, design, obtaining permits, and construction. Once the job is done, I teach people how to operate the system. The whole process can take several years.

Water-system installation is a two-step process. First, we select a site for the city wells, and second, we build the whole system. This includes drilling the wells, constructing storage and treatment facilities, and putting in the water mains (large pipes that carry water).

In selecting the site for Charlestown's wells, we had to stay uphill from the gasoline plume and drill deeply enough to hit clean water.

To drill enough wells to supply a town, you have to estimate the town's current and future water needs. For Charlestown, we assumed that the population would increase by about 1,500 over the next 20 years, and then we determined how many wells were needed to meet the future water requirement. We decided three wells would do the job.

I got into this line of work through my interest in science. When I was in high school, I loved science, so in college, I majored in biology. Field biology was my favorite part of my studies. After college I worked as an operator at different waste-water treatment plants. When I discovered I was really interested in the environmental field, I decided to go to graduate school and get a master's degree in environmental engineering.

If you're interested in environmental engineering, you should take classes in engineering and in sciences such as biology and chemistry. I am amazed at how often biological and chemical principles provide clues that help me solve engineering problems.

I am one of those lucky people who loves going to work. My job gives me the opportunity to do the things I like to do, and help people at the same time.

The Dynamics of Groundwater

When you hear the word water you probably picture a clear lake, a flowing river, or a glass of cool water. You may be surprised to find out that most of the fresh water on our planet lies beneath your feet, where you can't see it. In fact, groundwater makes up ninety-seven percent (97%) of all fresh water in liquid form.

We rely on groundwater without thinking about it. Approximately one-fourth of all fresh water used in the U.S. comes from groundwater. Rural communities obtain ninety-five percent (95%) of their drinking water from underground sources. In urban areas, groundwater, whether from a public water-supply system or directly from a private well, provides about thirty-five percent (35%) of the drinking water supply.

Groundwater exists in a variety of forms. It can take the shape of confined underground lakes or moving streams that wind through underground caves or tunnels, but most groundwater exists in tiny spaces, or *pores*, in the soils and rocks underground. Most groundwater is located in loose sedimentary layers, but porous and fractured rocks hold much groundwater as well.

You may find it hard to imagine that rocks can hold water, but if you looked at a piece of limestone or sandstone under a microscope, you would see that it's full of empty spaces, tiny holes, cracks, and larger holes that can hold groundwater.

Rain, snow only a tiny share of world's water

When snow is piling up or rain is pouring down, it's easy to imagine that the air contains a good share of the Earth's water. But all the water vapor in the air, all the clouds and all the falling rain and snow add up to a small portion of Earth's water.

If all the water on Earth filled a 55-gallon drum, here's how it would be divided:

Oceans
53.39 gallons

Other
Including rivers
and lakes
1.1 ounces

Icecaps
and
glaciers
1.09
gallons

Under-
ground
.34 gallon

Atmosphere
.16 gallon

Source: U.S. Geological Survey

By Sam Ward, USA TODAY

Limestone and sandstone are sedimentary rocks. If you or your teacher has a piece of porous rock, experiment to see how much water it can absorb.

Different materials can hold different amounts of water. *Porosity* is the measure of the amount of space in a material available to hold groundwater. Loose sand and gravel have high porosity, while rocks have lower porosity. Porosity is one factor that determines whether rocks or sediments are good sources of groundwater. Permeability is also a factor.

Permeability is a measure of how easily water can move through pores within soil or rock. Permeability depends on the size of the pores and how

they are connected. For example, some rocks have high porosity but low permeability because the spaces where the water would be stored are physically separated from each other.

Groundwater is stored in sections of rock and soil called *aquifers* (which means "water-carriers"). Some aquifers are long, narrow strips, while others cover thousands of square miles underground. Aquifers may lie just below the surface of the earth or they may lie hundreds of feet deep. The depth of water in aquifers can also be just a few feet or hundreds of feet deep.

The quality of water in an aquifer may vary just as the amount can. It may be "new" water—from recent rains—or very "old" water—known as *fossil water*—which has been trapped in the earth for hundreds of years. You don't find aquifers only in wet places. There is a very large aquifer under the Sahara Desert!

An aquifer may be *confined*, which means that its top and bottom are made of impermeable rock, or *unconfined*, which means it is exposed to open air. The top of an unconfined aquifer is called the *water table*. Since confined aquifers trap water between two layers of impermeable rock, the water is under pressure. When a well is drilled through the top layer of a confined aquifer, the trapped water comes to the surface with great force, and is called an *artesian well*.

Capillarity

Even when left undisturbed, groundwater does not stay in one place. Through a process called *capillarity*, or capillary action, it creeps from one pore to another. Capillarity is the ability of a liquid to move through a solid. It can even defy the pull of gravity and move upward. During its movement through the soil, water is usually cleansed by microorganisms. These microorganisms filter out or break down some types of foreign matter and contaminants.

Groundwater may move from just a fraction of an inch a year to as much as a few feet in a day. It may take centuries for a drop of water to make its way from the spot where it seeped into the aquifer to a *discharge area*, the place where groundwater naturally enters a lake or stream.

Underground Gasoline Tanks

Gas stations in the United States use more than a million underground storage tanks. Most of these tanks are quite old, and many were installed in the 1950s or earlier. The great majority of them are made of steel. Steel rusts, and when it does, the tank will leak. Between five and six million underground storage tanks are used to store a variety of materials. In addition to storing gasoline, they are used to store fuel oil and numerous chemicals.

According to the U.S. Environmental Protection Agency, steel tanks begin to leak after an average of 18 years; leaks in connective piping to the tanks usually occur even sooner. It is estimated that every year several hundred thousand to millions of gallons of gasoline and other chemicals leak from storage tanks into the ground and eventually into our aquifers.

Why do some underground storage tanks leak, while others do not? Tanks may have been improperly installed, or corrosion (rust) may have occurred because of moisture in the soil and inside the tank. Corrosion may also be caused by the difference in the metals used for the tank and the piping, or by electrochemical reactions between the metal of the tank and the soil. Even electric power lines buried nearby can contribute to tank corrosion.

Problems occur in the piping system at least sixty percent (60%) more often than with the tanks themselves. Pipes may leak as a result of improper alignment, corrosion, or stress due to freezing or thawing.

Natural disasters like earthquakes, tornadoes, hurricanes, and floods can also cause leaks. Underground storage tanks present an unusual dilemma to communities faced with flooding. Tanks can break if the water table rises and pressure forces them upwards. The buoyancy of the tank—especially with air trapped inside when it is not full—can even cause it to break through the ground and float. It was not until the mid-1980s that the Environmental Protection Agency began investigating leaky underground storage tanks. Since then, the installation of new tanks has been carefully regulated, old tanks are closely monitored, and owners of leaky tanks are held legally responsible.

Federal regulations require that new tanks must be made either of a steel composite with a fiberglass-reinforced plastic shell; coated and electrically-protected steel; or fiberglass-reinforced plastic.

Piping systems are now available with dual-wall flexible pipes encased in electrically protected containers. These new systems are not only protected from corrosion, they also will keep a leak from spreading and send a warning signal to the tank owner. Monitoring and shut-off systems are also available.

A Day's Worth of Water

Purpose

To calculate the amount of water your family and your "town" uses over a period of time.

Background

Charlestown must make a decision about its municipal water supply. In order for the town commissioners to make an informed decision, they need data. The commissioners need to know the total daily household water use for the entire town. Once they have this information, they will estimate the monthly and yearly water needs of Charlestown.

You and your science class have been asked to take part in collecting data. You will provide the commissioners with the daily water usage in your home. Since your house uses well water there is no water meter. To get an accurate estimate of your water use, you will keep a daily water-use log for three days. Using the data from those three days you will calculate your family's average daily water usage.

Materials

- Paper
- Liquid measuring devices found at home (for example, measuring cups, milk containers, marked pails)

Procedure

Get together with three or four of your neighbors and brainstorm a list of the different ways you use water around the house. Share your list with the class. Make a master list that combines your ideas with those of the other neighborhood groups. Take the items listed on your list and develop a daily water-use log.

Brainstorm a procedure that you and your family will follow to keep track of your daily water usage. Share your ideas with the class and add to your list as you did before. Be sure to think of methods for calculating the water flow from different types of faucets around your home. This will help you estimate the different types of data that you will need to keep in your log.

Brainstorm a way to obtain estimates of business water usage for your town.

Here are some questions to keep in mind as you prepare to present your results to your neighborhood group:

1. Based on your records, how much water will your family use over a 30 day period?
2. Based on your records, how much water will your family use over a year?
3. Were there any household water uses that were not included in your study? If yes, estimate how much water you need to add to your daily average if these other uses were taken into account.

Here are some questions to consider as your neighborhood group prepares its report:

4. How much water did the families in your neighborhood use over the 3 days?
5. How much water will be used by the families in your neighborhood during one month? One year?

Conclusion

Present your findings to your neighborhood group. Neatly prepared charts and graphs are essential for this presentation. Then, along with your neighbors, prepare a report showing major uses and the total quantity of water usage on your block. This information will be given to the commissioners to help them make estimate Charlestown's water usage.

Charlestown water project may cost about $3 million

By Kimberly Hook
Whig Staff Writer

Nearly 120 Charlestown residents learned Wednesday night about the town's plans to construct a $3 million water system.

A new town water system has been proposed for Charlestown for nearly 20 years, but the project has always been put off because of high costs.

This year, the town may not have a choice because most of the private, shallow wells that serve the town are contaminated with bacteria and some contain gasoline.

Robert Fisher, town administrator, said the Charlestown commissioners are expected to vote in a special session sometime in December or early January on whether to proceed with the project, which is estimated to cost $3,022,000.

Questionnaires distributed

Meanwhile, the town has distributed questionnaires asking townspeople if they support the project. A decision by the commissioners will follow analysis of the responses to the questionnaire, Fisher said, adding that most people seem to support the new system.

Some town commissioners are concerned that townspeople believe a new system is unaffordable and would not support it. Placing the issue on referendum in the town's upcoming January election was considered, but the town's charter only requires referendums for new ordinances.

To help defray costs, Fisher said the town is also considering serving the Charlestown Manor and Charlestown Beach areas -- residential communities bordering town limits. To do that, the town would probably require those communities to become part of the town's corporate limits through annexation. An estimated 500 new town residents would have to pay for use of the water system through water use charges. Town residents also pay town taxes.

If the town were to serve itself and the Charlestown Manor and Beach areas, the new system could cost $3,929,000. But, cost to the individual consumer could be less.

Fisher said that with no connection fee, service to the town and those two areas could cost the consumer $278. Service to the town and the Charlestown Beach area may cost $292.

With a $500 hookup fee, service to the town and the two areas could be $241. Again with a $500 fee, service to the town and Charlestown Beach could be $256 per year.

Fisher said the connection fee reduces the amount the town would need to borrow for the project, while the user fee repays the loan, pays for operation and maintenance. A portion of revenue from the user fee would also be reserved for any repairs the system might require in the future.

Gasoline problem update

Meanwhile, the Maryland Department of the Environment (MDE) is still paying for operation and maintenance of carbon filters to 20 residences in which water is contaminated with gasoline.

Robert DeMarco, chief of the state's Leaking Underground Storage Tank (LUST) Projects Division, said 3,501 gallons of free gasoline have been withdrawn from Charlestown's water supply.

The gasoline allegedly leaked from two underground gasoline storage tanks from the Trading Postmarket. The leaking tank was removed in 1987. The state is currently seeking "cost recovery" from what are called potentially responsible parties.

DeMarco said the amount of free gasoline is tapering off. The state withdrew about 1,000 gallons per month and has been withdrawing about 20 gallons per month since.

He said the state will continue to operate its withdrawal system for as long as it takes to remove the free product, but the state has hired a consultant to determine alternatives for removing dissolved gasoline from Charlestown's water supply.

R. E. Wright Associates Inc. has prepared a range of alternatives, DeMarco said, explaining that the state is seeking design proposals from engineers for the best system to remove the dissolved gasoline. He said engineers will have about 120 days to submit proposals and one of those is expected to be bid sometime in January.

CECIL WHIG, DECEMBER 3, 1988

Math: Leaks and Volume

Purpose
To determine whether or not a gasoline storage tank has a leak.

Procedure
You and your partner own a small gas station. Recently, water in some nearby wells has become contaminated. The State Department of the Environment investigated the well and believes that one or more of your underground gasoline storage tanks may be leaking. They have asked you to review your records and then confirm or deny the charges in writing. Criminal charges will be filed if you fail to act promptly and honestly.

These two diagrams came with the tanks.

You and your partner have decided to use manual gauging to determine whether any leaks exist. On Monday, a measuring pole is lowered into each tank to determine the height of the gasoline. The regular tank has gasoline in it at a level of 18 feet, while the premium tank has a level of 14 feet. On Saturday, another measurement is taken and the regular tank's level is 10 feet, while the premium tank has a level of 8 feet. During that time, 4,700 gallons of regular gas and 1,930 gallons of premium gas were sold. Use your measurements and the formula below to determine if any leaks exist. (Note: 1 cubic foot = 7.48 gallons)

$$V = \pi(r^2 \times h)$$

The volume of a cylinder is equal to 3.14 times the product of the radius squared and the height (when $\pi = 3.14$).

State your conclusion in a letter to
Gloria Weller
Director, Water Testing
Department of the Environment
Be sure to include the results from your measurement experiment to justify your conclusion.

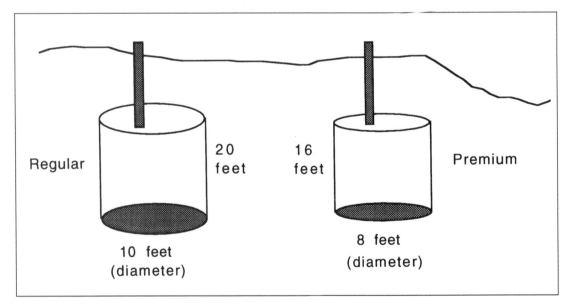

Regular   20 feet   16 feet   Premium

10 feet
(diameter)

8 feet
(diameter)

Social Studies: Hazardous Waste, a National Problem

Purpose

You have been chosen to be part of a team studying the location of hazardous waste sites in the United States. The U.S. Environmental Protection Agency has identified 1,201 hazardous waste sites. Your task is to make a detailed study of waste sites in one state. Based on your findings, identify the industry(s) responsible for creation of these sites, and describe the impact that these sites are having on the people of the state.

Materials

- Atlas
- Encyclopedias
- Almanac
- Hazardous Waste Site Information by State, page 45
- colored pencils
- poster paper

Procedure

Using the information provided by your teacher, you are to create a color-coded map of the United States that shows the number of hazardous waste sites by state. The map must have a legend that is developed according to guidelines also provided by the teacher.

Once your map is completed, select an individual state to investigate further. (Your teacher may choose to assign a specific state.)

On a piece of poster paper, draw a large map of the state you are investigating; color the state the same color as it appeared on the map; and show the locations of hazardous waste sites within that state.

Using an encyclopedia, an almanac, and an atlas, locate and label the 10 largest cities found within the state on your map.

Include the following information on your poster: total population of the state; total area; population density (population per square mile); total population rank (when compared to the other 49 states); and total area rank (when compared to the other 49 states).

Identify the major industries located within the state. Create small pictures that represent each of these industries and draw these pictures on your map.

Using the information you have gathered about your state (area, population, population density, major industries, bordering states), write a brief report explaining the impact of hazardous waste sites on the people living in this state. If your state has few hazardous waste sites, explain why the state's population is not threatened by hazardous waste. Keep in mind that your state borders other states that have additional hazardous waste sites. In your report, mention the impact that hazardous waste sites in neighboring states could have upon your state's population.

Writing to Persuade

Directions
Complete the writing activity below. Read the prompt carefully. You may refer to all your previous work in this unit.

Prompt
You have concluded your investigation of your community's water supply problems. You are now being asked to recommend a site for a community well and to propose the best plan for a municipal water supply. You need to write a business letter to the town commissioners in which you describe the site you've chosen and defend your plan for the new municipal water supply.

Before you begin writing, review the details of your investigation: What are the problems that have caused your community's water crisis? What is the best site for a community well? What evidence can you present to defend the site you have selected? Who will pay for the new well and water delivery system? What are the long-term benefits? Can you foresee any disadvantages? How can you effectively persuade the town commissioners to adopt your plan?

Now, write a business letter to the town commissioners in which you select, explain, and defend your plan for the new municipal water supply. As you write, ask yourself the following questions:

1. Have you clearly presented and explained your site and plan?
2. Have you included all the details necessary to gain acceptance for your position?
3. Have you written appropriately to your intended audience, the town commissioners?
4. Have you used evidence and logic to persuade?
5. Have you followed correct business-letter format?
6. Have you proofread and edited your letter? (Use the Proofreading Guidesheet on page 40.)

Have your peers evaluate and react to your letter, using the Peer-Response Form on page 39.

Peer-Response Form

Directions

1. Ask your partners to listen carefully as you read your rough draft aloud.

2. Ask your partners to help you improve your writing by telling you the answers to the questions below.

3. Jot down notes about what your partners say.

    a. What did you like best about my rough draft?

    b. What did you have the hardest time understanding about my rough draft?

    c. What can you suggest that I do to improve my rough draft?

4. Exchange rough drafts with a partner. In pencil, place a check mark near any mechanical, spelling, or grammatical constructions about which you are uncertain. Return the papers and check your own. Ask your partner for clarification if you do not understand or agree with the comments on your paper. Jot down notes you will want to remember when writing your revision.

Proofreading Guidesheet

1. Have you identified the assigned purpose of the writing assignment and have you accomplished that purpose?

2. Have you written on the assigned topic?

3. Have you identified the assigned form your writing should take and written accordingly?

4. Have you addressed the assigned audience in your writing?

5. Have you used sentences of different lengths and types to make your writing effective?

6. Have you chosen language carefully so the reader understands what you mean?

7. Have you done the following to make your writing clear for someone else to read:

   - used appropriate capitalization?
   - kept pronouns clear?
   - kept verb tense consistent?
   - made sure all words are spelled correctly?
   - used correct punctuation?
   - used complete sentences?
   - made all subjects and verbs agree?
   - organized your ideas into logical paragraphs?

Gasoline

What Is It?

Gasoline is one of our most important transportation fuels. Gasoline is a valuable and irreplaceable natural resource that results from the refinement of *petroleum*, or crude oil. (In Latin *petra* means rock and *oleum* is oil.) We use gasoline to power automobiles, trucks, and numerous other machines. In most cities and towns, gasoline is easily available. Many towns have three or four gas stations within a single block.

Petroleum has been used since ancient times. According to the Bible, Noah used *pitch*—a black oil that seeps from the ground—to make his ark watertight. *Eternal fires*, crude oil seepages that were ignited by lightning, have been revered by different peoples throughout history. Most petroleum, though, is found deep underground, beyond our reach, where it was formed millions of years ago.

Why Do We Use Gasoline as a Fuel?

Crude oil began to be used as a fuel in the middle of the nineteenth century in response to the invention of the kerosene lamp. Before kerosene, whale oil was burned in lamps. People also produced light by burning candles, which use animal fat as their fuel. In those early days of oil production, gasoline was simply dumped as a useless by-product of kerosene production.

The 1890s saw the introduction of the internal combustion engine, which generates power by burning a spray of fine gasoline droplets ignited by an electric spark. The first "horseless carriage" with a gasoline engine appeared in the late 1800s. By 1908, Henry Ford had started production of the Model T, the first automobile priced cheaply enough for ordinary people to afford. As automobiles became available to more and more people, the need for gasoline increased. That need has climbed steadily ever since.

Today when you pull into a gas station, you see different *grades,* or qualities, of gasoline. The grading system expresses the anti-knock quality of the gasoline in terms of its octane level. Knocking occurs when gasoline ignites too early, causing a repeated "ping" or knocking sound as the car accelerates. High-performance engines require higher octane gasoline. Higher octane gasoline burns more slowly and resists pre-ignition. Of course, the higher the octane rating, the more expensive the gasoline.

Until just a few years ago, lead was added to gasoline to reduce engine knock. But leaded gasoline is being phased out because people fear the negative consequences of breathing the lead in automobile exhaust.

Our need for gasoline and other oil products has serious environmental costs. Air pollution is a result of our over-dependence on gasoline-powered vehicles and also of oil refineries. Oil-tanker spills and even routine maintenance practices, such as flushing out tanks at sea, foul the ocean, destroy beaches, and kill birds and other marine life. The used motor oil that people discard carelessly is a major cause of ground and water pollution. And, as you are learning in this module, gasoline is one of the greatest threats to our groundwater.

Where Does It Come From?

Scientists have found evidence that oil was formed from the bodies of the tiny plants and animals that lived and died in ancient seas and swamps. Over thousands of years, the bodies of these plants and animals formed gooey deposits on the floors of their swamp and sea homes. Eventually they were buried by mud and sand deposited over them. In some places under these layers of sediment oxygen was not available, so dead plants and animals did not decay completely. Instead they decomposed into a slimy mass.

Millions of years passed, and more and more layers of sediment were laid down over the decomposing organisms. These sediments eventually cemented together to form the porous rocks we call sandstone and limestone. The fats and oils from the bodies of these partially decayed prehistoric creatures slowly became the oil and natural gas we value so highly today. The oil moved through tiny pores in the rocks as if through a sponge, until it came to an impermeable (nonporous) layer of rock which formed a barrier. There the oil and gasoline accumulated as if in a trap.

Deposits of crude oil are found as underground oil pools, oil sands, and oil shales. Deposits are found on every continent and in many offshore seabeds. About two-thirds of Earth's known oil reserves have been found in the Middle East. Oil reserves in Europe and Asia represent only about seven percent (7%) of the world's oil supply. Latin America, especially Venezuela and Mexico, has oil reserves representing about twelve percent (12%) of the world's total supply. The United States and Canada together have about three percent (3%) of that total. Most of the U.S. reserves are found in Texas, Louisiana, Oklahoma, California, and Alaska.

In spite of its current availability, the supply of petroleum will not last forever! The quantity of oil on Earth is limited. If we continue to use it at our current rates, we will eventually use it all up. Conservation makes sense for this reason alone, but there is another reason to conserve gasoline and other petroleum products: Burning them is hazardous to our health. The carbon dioxide that is released into the atmosphere when petroleum products are burned is a greenhouse gas. That means it may be contributing to global warming. Also, the

carbon monoxide exhausted from automobiles pollutes the air.

Much is being done in industrialized countries to reduce the consumption of oil. Designing more fuel-efficient cars and machines and using these machines more wisely are two successful methods for conserving. We must try to be wise in our use of oil.

What Is Crude Oil?

Crude oil is a mixture of many chemical compounds. Chief among them are compounds called *hydrocarbons*, which contain only atoms of hydrogen and carbon. Some hydrocarbons have

carbon

hydrogen

just a few carbon atoms, while others have thousands of them linked together in long chains. The more carbon atoms a molecule contains, the heavier and thicker the hydrocarbon. Through the process of petroleum distillation, hydrocarbons with similar structures and properties are removed from the crude oil.

For example, the black gooey asphalt used for paving streets is an extract of the heavy hydrocarbons found in crude oil. Kerosene, which is much lighter than asphalt, is an extract of shorter, lighter hydrocarbons. Gasoline is a mixture of hydrocarbons with five to eleven carbon atoms in each molecule.

What are the properties of gasoline that make it so useful? First, it is light, free-flowing, and

can be stored easily. Second, it forms a gas, or vaporizes easily, at ordinary temperatures. Third, and most importantly, gasoline is a highly flammable liquid. A light, highly flammable fuel was just what was needed in the late nineteenth century with the invention of that very important machine, the internal combustion engine.

Gasoline Safety

Handling gasoline, whether in large or small quantities, requires certain safety precautions. The useful features of gasoline—its high flammability and its easy vaporization—are also dangerous features. For example, when storing gasoline in a gas can, never place the can near sources of heat, such as lighted matches, because the fumes ignite easily. Gas cans should never be carried inside a car because gasoline vapors are intoxicating. Breathing them in could possibly impair the driver's coordination and reaction time.

Gasoline is especially dangerous in an car accident. When gasoline flows from a punctured tank, it can be ignited by sparks from steel grinding against concrete. This explosive combination is familiar to anyone who has seen car chases in the movies. These explosions can happen in real life, too. No matter what quantity of gasoline you happen to be around, whether a small amount in a gas can or a large amount in a gasoline tanker truck, never forget the dangers.

Using what you know now about gasoline, can you explain why an almost-empty gas can is more likely to explode than a full one?

Household Hazardous Waste Chart

Some waste materials require more careful disposal while others may simply be poured down a drain with lots of water. Some materials that cannot be poured down a drain may be disposed of in a sanitary landfill; some otherwise hazardous waste can be recycled; and certain wastes must only be disposed of by licensed hazardous-waste contractors. Perhaps your community holds special collection days for these wastes.

Origin	Type of Waste	Appropriate Method of Disposal			
		Hazardous Waste	Landfill	Safe to Pour Down the Drain	Recyclable
Kitchen	Aerosol cans, empty		X		
	Aluminum cleaners			X	
	Ammonia-based cleaners			X	
	Bug sprays	X			
	Drain cleaners			X	
	Floor-care products	X			
	Furniture polish	X			
	Metal polish with solvent	X			
	Window cleaner			X	
	Oven cleaner, lye-based		X		
Bathroom	Alcohol-based lotions (aftershaves, perfumes, etc.)			X	
	Bathroom cleaners			X	
	Depilatories (hair removers)			X	
	Disinfectants			X	
	Permanent			X	
	Hair relaxers			X	
	Medicine, expired			X	
	Nail polish, solidified		X		
	Toilet bowl cleaner			X	
	Tub and tile cleaners			X	
Garage	Antifreeze	X			X
	Automatic transmission fluid	X			X
	Auto-body repair products		X		
	Battery acid (or battery)	X			X
	Brake fluid	X			
	Car wax with solvent	X			
	Diesel fuel	X			X
	Fuel oil	X			X
	Gasoline	X			X

Origin	Type of Waste	Hazardous Waste	Landfill	Safe to Pour Down the Drain	Recyclable
Garage	Kerosene	X			X
	Metal polish with solvent	X			
	Motor oil	X			X
	Other oils	X			
	Windshield-washer solution			X	
Workshop	Paintbrush cleaner with solvent	X			X
	Paintbrush cleaner with TSP			X	
	Aerosol cans, empty		X		
	Cutting oil	X			
	Glue, solvent based	X			
	Glue, water based			X	
	Paint, latex		X		
	Paint, oil based	X			
	Paint, auto	X			
	Paint, model	X			
	Paint thinner	X			X
	Paint stripper	X			
	Paint stripper, lye-based			X	
	Primer	X			
	Rust remover, with phosphoric acid			X	
	Turpentine	X			X
	Varnish	X			
	Wood preservative	X			
Garden	Fertilizer		X		
	Fungicide	X			
	Herbicide	X			
	Insecticide	X			
	Rat poison	X			
	Weed killer	X			
Miscellaneous	Ammunition (bullets and so on)	X			
	Artists' paints, mediums	X			
	Dry-cleaning solvents	X			X
	Fiberglass epoxy	X			
	Gun-cleaning solvents	X			X
	Lighter fluid	X			
	Mercury batteries	X			
	Moth balls	X			
	Old fire alarms	X			
	Photographic chemicals, unmixed	X			
	Photographic chemicals, mixed and properly diluted			X	
	Shoe polish		X		
	Swimming pool acid	X			

This chart is based on material published by the Water Environment Federation, 601 Wythe Street, Alexandria, VA 22314-1944.

Designated Hazardous Waste Sites by State

State	Count	State	Count	State	Count
Alabama	12	Maine	9	Oregon	8
Alaska	8	Maryland	10	Pennsylvania	97
Arizona	10	Massachusetts	25	Rhode Island	12
Arkansas	10	Michigan	77	South Carolina	23
California	91	Minnesota	42	South Dakota	4
Colorado	16	Mississippi	2	Tennessee	14
Connecticut	15	Missouri	22	Texas	29
Delaware	15	Montana	8	Utah	12
Florida	52	Nebraska	8	Vermont	8
Georgia	15	Nevada	1	Virginia	20
Hawaii	2	New Hampshire	17	Washington	29
Idaho	9	New Jersey	109	West Virginia	5
Illinois	37	New Mexico	10	Wisconsin	39
Indiana	33	New York	84	Wyoming	3
Iowa	20	North Carolina	22		
Kansas	11	North Dakota	2		
Kentucky	9	Ohio	33	Source: *Statistical Abstract of the*	
Louisiana	11	Oklahoma	10	*United States.*	

Water Facts

From a land dweller's perspective, our planet can appear to be a relatively dry place to live, but, in fact, water covers about seventy-five percent (75%) of Earth's surface. The salty oceans hold about ninety-seven percent (97%) of all surface water; another two percent is locked in ice caps and glaciers.

Vast amounts of fresh water lie under Earth's surface, but much of it is too deep to reach economically. Amazingly, less than one-half of one percent of Earth's water is available as fresh water in the form of groundwater, lakes, and rivers.

When early settlers established the first farms and towns, they made their homes in river valleys and other regions where a reliable source of water was available. Waterways were also important to them as avenues of transportation.

We see the same patterns in our industrialized modern society. Industries have located their facilities on rivers and lakes not only because of the transportation benefits for distributing raw materials and finished products, but also because they want to take advantage of the water to cool their machinery. A great concern today is the water pollution that often results from these industries.

Water Molecules

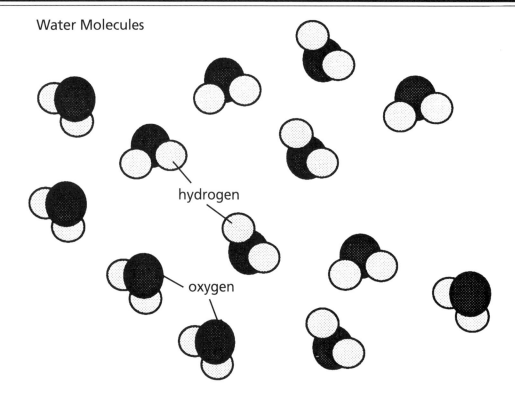

hydrogen

oxygen

Approximately one-fourth of all fresh water in the United States comes from groundwater. Industry uses about thirty percent (30%) of all groundwater, according to a 1990 report by the U.S. Environmental Protection Agency. More than one-third of all groundwater is used for agricultural purposes.

Life began in water, and is the basis of life as we know it. Water makes up about seventy-eight percent (78%) of our weight when we are born. As we grow older, the ratio of water to other substances in our bodies decreases as our bones and tissues develop, leaving our bodies at about sixty-five percent (65%) water as adults.

What Is Water?

Pure water is made up only of water molecules. A molecule of water is the smallest particle of water that exists. There are billions of them in a single drop of water. Each molecule of water is made up of two atoms of hydrogen (H) and one atom of oxygen (O)—the chemical compound called H_2O. When these atoms are combined together as H_2O, they act in different ways than how they act alone. For example, when hydrogen exists alone, is highly explosive; and when oxygen exists alone, it supports combustion. Yet together they form water, H_2O, which we use to extinguish fires!

Water: Liquid, Solid, and Gas

Water can be found in three physical states—liquid, solid and gas. Liquid water molecules stick together, roll over each other, and bump into each other. Water in its liquid state conforms to the shape of its container. When you put liquid water in the freezer, though, the molecules begin to act differently. As the water's temperature drops, the molecules stop rolling and tumbling. The molecules in frozen water, or ice, are locked into place in patterns called *crystals*.

As liquid water is heated, a different process happens. Molecules move faster and faster as they absorb heat, and they transform the heat energy into an energy of rapid motion. When you boil water, some water molecules begin to move quickly enough to escape into the air as *water vapor*, or steam, leaving behind any chemicals or impurities. You can see this residue left behind on the pan after the water boils away. When water vapor is cooled and collected, it is known as *distilled water*.

Water in the Environment

Water can be fresh or salty (or *brackish*, which means slightly salty), hard or soft, spring or carbonated, clean or polluted. We encounter it in various forms—liquid, solid, and gas—in different environments. Liquid water is found in rivers, streams, lakes, seas, oceans, rain, and under ground. Droplets of liquid water also show up as clouds and fog. We find frozen water falling as snow, sleet, and hail, or slowly flowing as glaciers in polar and some mountainous regions. Invisible water vapor is always present in the air as something called *humidity*.

It had been thought that seawater is salty because the salt minerals that dissolved from rocks were washed by rain into rivers and then were carried into oceans. Eventually, over thousands of years, the oceans would have become saltier and saltier as more minerals were deposited there. This theory has now been displaced by evidence that the concentration of salts and minerals in the oceans is controlled by releases from the sea floor itself.

The difference between hard and soft water is easy to explain. Hard water has a high content of such minerals as calcium and magnesium. Hard water leaves a deposit on the surfaces it touches. Bathtubs, sinks, pipes, and faucets often become encrusted. It is also difficult to work up a lather with soap in hard water. Water can be softened by adding lime and soda ash, and then filtering the water.

Polluted water can be hard or soft, fresh or salty. Potential water pollutants are numerous, but most fall into the following groups:

- Biological: Parasites, bacteria, viruses, and other living microorganisms generally enter the water supply via human sewage.

- Inorganic chemicals: Some examples include cyanide, fluoride, and lead. Though these occur naturally in all water in small amounts, when they become concentrated as in mining and processing, these chemicals are hazardous.

- Radioactive elements: These exist at low levels in nature, but nuclear power plants and the mining of uranium for these plants have increased their presence in the waterways.

- Fertilizers: Nitrogen and phosphorous that come from agricultural and lawn fertilizers. These cause rapid growth of bacteria and algae in the waterways into which they drain. Sewage also contributes to the buildup of nitrogen.

- Organic chemicals: Carbon compounds find their way into waterways. Examples include artificial substances, such as industrial solvents and pesticides, and naturally occurring carbon compounds, including fats and oils.

Drinking Water

In most areas of this country, we simply turn on a faucet to get our drinking water—water that our city and county governments assure us is safe. But in many parts of the world, clean drinking water is hard to find. In developing countries, people are often forced to carry water for miles. The lack of clean, unpolluted water is a major factor in the high incidence of disease and the high infant mortality rates in these countries.

Even though tap water is safe for drinking in the industrialized world, bottled water is popular for reasons of taste and health. Many people believe that the minerals contained in bottled drinking water are essential to good health. A bottle of water labeled *natural* may be from a well, a spring, or another source. The word *natural* also tells you that the water has not been changed during packaging. *Spring water* on a label refers specifically to water that comes from a spring. "Spring water" might be processed before bottling, but "natural spring water" is not. Sparkling water, including brands like Perrier®, is carbonated, which means it contains dissolved carbon dioxide. It may be either naturally sparkling or artificially carbonated during bottling.

Water: The Universal Solvent

Scientists have called water the *universal solvent*. Its chemical makeup *dissolves*, or breaks apart, many substances, causing them to form *solutions*. This property of water to dissolve and carry substances in solution explains its importance to us. Water carries needed minerals and nutrients throughout our bodies, and it also carries away waste chemicals.

However, since water can dissolve substances so readily, it is easily polluted beyond nature's ability to clean it. Throughout the world, rivers and lakes are being pushed to their limits. Sometimes they are unable to dissolve what is otherwise "biodegradable" waste. In addition, pollutants that are not biodegradable continue to be put in our rivers, oceans, and lakes. It is easy to understand why our water supplies are at risk.

BIBLIOGRAPHY

Adler, Irving. *Petroleum: Gas, Oil and Asphalt*. New York: The John Day Company, 1975.

Cobb, Vicki. *The Trip of a Drip*. Boston: Little, Brown and Company, 1986.

Doty, Roy. *Where Are You Going with that Oil?* Garden City, New York: Doubleday, 1976.

Hoff, Mary, and Mary Rodgers. *Our Endangered Planet: Groundwater*. Minneapolis: Lerner Publications, 1991.

Lambert, David, and Diagram Group Staff. *The Field Guide to Geology*. New York: Facts On File, 1989.

Lambert, Mark. *Spotlight on Oil*. Vero Beach, Florida: Rourke Enterprises, Inc., 1986.

National Geographic Society. *Water: The Power, Promise, and Turmoil of North America's Fresh Water*. (National Geographic Special Edition), Vol. 184, No. 5A, November 1993.

O'Neill, Mary. *Water Squeeze*, The SOS Planet Earth Series. Mahwah, New Jersey: Troll Associates, 1989.

Roberts, W.G. *The Quest for Oil*. London: Methuen and Co., 1970.

Seed, Deborah. *Water Science*. Reading, Massachusetts: Addison-Wesley Publishing Co., Inc., 1992.

Stahl, Nancy N., and Robert J. Stahl. *Society and Science: Decision-Making Episodes for Exploring Society, Science, and Technology*. Menlo Park, Calif.: Addison-Wesley Publishing Co., Inc., 1995.

Stewart, John C. *Drinking Water Hazards: How to Know If There Are Toxic Chemicals in Your Water and What to Do If There Are*. Hiram, Ohio: Envirographics, 1990.

U.S. Environmental Protection Agency, Office of Ground-Water Protection. *Citizen's Guide To Ground-Water Protection*. (# EPA 440/6-90-004) Washington, D.C.: U.S. Government Printing Office, April 1990.

World Resources Institute Staff. *The 1994 Information Please Environmental Almanac*. Boston: Houghton Mifflin, 1993.

Acknowledgments

Author
Russell G. Wright, with contributions from Leonard David and Barbara Sprungman and the following teachers:

*Nancy A. Carey, Col. E. Brooke Lee Middle School, Silver Spring, MD
*Charles E. Doebler, Robert Frost Middle School, Rockville, MD
*Bernard J. Hudock, Watkins Mill High School, Gaithersburg, MD
*Nell Jeter, Earle B. Wood Middle School, Rockville, MD
*Cynthia Johnson-Cash, Ridgeview Middle School, Gaithersburg, MD
*Jeanne S. Klugel, Col. E. Brooke Lee Middle School, Silver Spring, MD
*Harry P. Mazur, Parkland Middle School, Rockville, MD
*Eugene M. Molesky, Ridgeview Middle School, Gaithersburg, MD
*Joseph M. Panarella, Montgomery Village Middle School, Gaithersburg, MD
*John Senuta, Ridgeview Intermediate School, Gaithersburg, MD
*J. Martin Smiley ,Gaithersburg Intermediate School, Gaithersburg, MD
*Thomas G. Smith, Briggs Chaney Middle School, Silver Spring, MD
*Frank S. Weisel, Poolesville Junior/Senior High School, Poolesville, MD
Evan D. Wolff, University of Maryland, College Park, MD

Event/Site Support
Judy Kidd, Monroe, North Carolina

Scientific Reviewers
Dorothy K. Hall, L. Walter, Dave Stevens, Charles Boyle, and Nahid Khazenie, National Aeronautics and Space Administration

Student Consultants
*Redland Middle School, Rockville, MD
Nathan Unce, Daniel Weimer, Melissa Mong, Roxanna Nwachukwu, Sommer Yirka, Genevieve Maricle, Brian Houska, Gloria Lee, Lise Hyon, Ethan Lee, Rebecca Marshall, Laura Downing, Halima Karzai, Alison Dean, Erick Carlson, Erin Kerman, Jereme Price, Lawrence Matthews, Jr., Anne Kiang, Nina Armah, Becky Richardson, Luis Castro, Monique Frazier, Crystal Shirley, Laura-Marie Armstrong, Gina Romano, Paul Hayes, Jr.
*Ridgeview Intermediate School, Gaithersburg, MD
Sean Shillinger

Field-Test Teachers
Judith Basile and Karen Shugrue, Agawam Junior High School, Feeding Hills, MA
David Needham and Gloria Yost, Albert Einstein Middle School, Sacramento, CA
Annette Newsome, West Baltimore Middle School, Baltimore, MD
Joanne Cannon and Adrianne Criminger, Lanier Middle School, Buford, GA
Cheryl Glotfelty and Von Mosser, Northern Middle School, Accident, MD
Mark Carlson and Mary Ridenour, Westlane Middle School, Indianapolis, IN

EBS Advisory Committee
Dr. Eddie Anderson, National Aeronautic and Space Administration
Ms. Mary Ann Brearton, American Association for the Advancement of Science
Dr. Lynn Dierking, National Museum of American History
Mr. Bob Dubill, *USA Today*

Mr. Herbert Freiberger, United States Geological Survey
Ms. Joyce Gross, National Oceanic and Atmospheric Administration
Dr. Harry Herzer, National Aeronautic and Space Administration
Mr. Frank Ireton, American Geophysical Union
*Mr. Bill Krayer, Gaithersburg High School
Dr. Ivo Lindauer, National Science Foundation
Dr. Rocky Lopes, American Red Cross
*Dr. Jerry Lynch, John T. Baker Middle School
Ms. Virginia Major, United States Geological Survey
Ms. Marilyn P. MacCabe, Federal Emergency management Agency
Mr. John Ortman, United States Department of Energy
Dr. Noel Raufasté, Jr., National Institute of Standards and Technology
Dr. Bill Sacco, Trianalytics Corporation
Mr. Ron Slotkin, United States Environmental Protection Agency
Ms. Katarina Stenstedt, Addison-Wesley Publishing Co.

*Montgomery County Public Schools